New Jersey Real Estate License Exam: Best Test Prep Book to Help You Get Your License!

The Ultimate Workbook: Salesperson and Broker Exam-Passing Strategies

Table of Content

Introduction

If you're holding this book, chances are you're on the cusp of embarking on an exciting journey into the world of real estate in the Garden State—New Jersey. Whether you're a complete novice with a newfound interest in real estate or a seasoned professional looking to expand your horizons, "New Jersey Real Estate Learning - New Jersey Real Estate License Exam: Best Test Prep Book to Help You Get Your License!" is designed to be your comprehensive guide. This book aims to equip you with the knowledge, skills, and strategies you'll need to not only pass the New Jersey Real Estate License Exam but also to thrive in this dynamic and rewarding industry.

Why New Jersey?

New Jersey offers a unique blend of opportunities for real estate professionals. With its proximity to major cities like New York and Philadelphia, diverse landscapes ranging from bustling urban centers to serene shorelines, and a robust economy, the state's real estate market is as varied as it is vibrant. Whether you're interested in residential, commercial, or industrial real estate, New Jersey has something for everyone. This book will delve into the specificities of the New Jersey real estate market, providing you with localized knowledge that will give you an edge in your career.

What This Book Covers

This book is structured to provide a step-by-step guide through all the stages of becoming a licensed real estate agent in New Jersey. From understanding the eligibility criteria and navigating the application process to mastering the laws and regulations that govern real estate practices in the state, we've got you covered. We'll also delve into the nitty-gritty details of property valuation, financing, contracts, and much more. Each chapter is designed to build on the previous one, ensuring a smooth learning curve.

Beyond the Exam

While the primary goal is to help you pass the New Jersey Real Estate License Exam, this book also aims to offer a holistic view of what a career in real estate entails. You'll find chapters dedicated to ethics, legal considerations, and career development. We'll discuss the importance of networking, choosing the right brokerage, and even touch upon how technology is shaping the future of real estate.

Practical Insights and Mock Exams

To ensure you're well-prepared, this book includes mock exams and practice questions modeled after the actual New Jersey Real Estate License Exam. These will give you a clear idea of what to expect and how to manage your time during the test. But we don't stop there; you'll also find practical tips and insights from industry experts to guide you beyond the exam room.

Your Companion for Success

Consider this book your comprehensive companion for success in the New Jersey real estate industry. As you turn each page, you'll gain valuable insights and practical knowledge that will serve you well, not just in your exam but throughout your career.

So, let's turn the page and take the first step together on your journey to becoming a licensed real estate agent in New Jersey. Welcome aboard!

Understanding the New Jersey Real Estate Market

Understanding the New Jersey real estate market is crucial for anyone aspiring to become a successful real estate agent in the state. The market is a complex ecosystem influenced by various factors such as economic conditions, housing demand and supply, and government policies. This chapter aims to provide a comprehensive overview of the New Jersey real estate market, covering its unique characteristics, key players, and trends that shape it.

Economic Overview

New Jersey is one of the most economically diverse states in the U.S., with strong sectors in pharmaceuticals, finance, technology, and tourism. Its strategic location, being close to major cities like New York and Philadelphia, adds to its economic strength. This diversity and strategic location significantly impact the real estate market, creating a wide range of opportunities for both residential and commercial real estate.

GDP and Employment

The state's GDP and employment rates are key indicators of its economic health, which in turn influences the real estate market. A strong economy often leads to increased demand for housing and commercial spaces. New Jersey has a robust economy with a GDP of around $634 billion as of 2021, making it one of the top 10 economies in the U.S. The state also boasts a lower unemployment rate compared to the national average, which positively impacts the real estate market.

Housing Market Trends

Home Prices and Sales

The New Jersey housing market has seen a steady increase in both home prices and sales over the past few years. The median home price in the state is around $400,000 as of 2022, with some areas like Hoboken and Jersey City experiencing even higher prices due to their proximity to New York City. The sales volume has also been robust, thanks to low mortgage rates and a strong economy.

Rental Market

The rental market in New Jersey is equally strong, especially in urban areas and those close to public transportation. The average rent for a one-bedroom apartment ranges from $1,200 to $2,500 depending on the location. Cities like Newark and Camden offer more affordable options, while Hoboken and Jersey City are on the pricier side.

Commercial Real Estate

Office Spaces

New Jersey offers a variety of options for businesses looking for office spaces. Cities like Newark and Jersey City are popular choices for corporations due to their proximity to New York City and better affordability. The demand for co-working spaces is also on the rise, influenced by the growing number of startups and freelancers.

Retail and Industrial Spaces

The state has a strong retail market, thanks to its affluent population and high population density. Malls and shopping centers are common in suburban areas, while high-street retail dominates the cities. The industrial real estate market is also robust, driven by New Jersey's strong manufacturing sector and its strategic location as a transportation hub.

Government Policies and Regulations

Understanding the legal landscape is crucial for real estate agents. New Jersey has specific laws and regulations that impact the real estate market, including property taxes, zoning laws, and rent control policies. For instance, New Jersey has one of the highest property taxes in the country, which can be a significant factor for homebuyers.

Future Trends

Technology in Real Estate

The adoption of technology is becoming increasingly prevalent in New Jersey's real estate market. Virtual tours, blockchain in property transactions, and AI-driven market analysis are some of the trends to watch.

Sustainability

Sustainable and green living is becoming more popular, influencing homebuyers and renters alike. Properties with energy-efficient features and proximity to public transportation are becoming increasingly desirable.

Conclusion

The New Jersey real estate market is a dynamic and complex entity, influenced by a myriad of factors ranging from economic conditions to technological advancements. For aspiring real estate agents, understanding this market is not just beneficial but essential for success. The market offers a plethora of opportunities in both residential and commercial sectors, making it a rewarding field for those who are well-prepared and informed.

Eligibility Criteria

Becoming a licensed real estate agent in New Jersey is a multi-step process that begins with meeting specific eligibility criteria. These criteria are set by the New Jersey Real Estate Commission and are designed to ensure that only qualified individuals enter the profession. This chapter will delve into the various eligibility requirements, including educational qualifications, age restrictions, background checks, and other essential factors that aspiring real estate agents must consider.

Age Requirements

Minimum Age

In New Jersey, the minimum age to apply for a real estate license is 18 years. This age requirement is pretty standard across most states and is considered the first eligibility criterion that aspiring agents must meet.

Age and Experience

While age is a factor, it's worth noting that real estate can be a career for people of all ages. Whether you're a young adult just starting or someone considering a career change later in life, the New Jersey real estate market is open to you as long as you meet the other eligibility criteria.

Educational Qualifications

High School Diploma or Equivalent

A high school diploma or its equivalent (such as a GED) is required to become a licensed real estate agent in New Jersey. This ensures that you have the basic educational foundation needed to understand and complete the required coursework and exams.

Pre-Licensing Education

Before applying for the license exam, you must complete 75 hours of pre-licensing education from a school approved by the New Jersey Real Estate Commission. This education covers various topics, including real estate law, ethics, and practices, and prepares you for the state licensing exam.

Legal Status

U.S. Citizenship or Legal Residency

You must be a U.S. citizen or a legal resident to apply for a real estate license in New Jersey. Non-citizens must provide proof of legal residency, such as a Green Card, to be considered eligible.

Criminal Background Check

A comprehensive criminal background check is mandatory for all applicants. The New Jersey Real Estate Commission will review your criminal history, if any, and may deny your application based on the findings. It's essential to disclose any criminal history honestly, as failure to do so can result in disqualification.

Financial Stability

Credit Score

While New Jersey does not have a specific credit score requirement, your financial stability may be assessed as part of the background check. A poor credit history could raise red flags but is generally not a disqualifying factor.

Bankruptcy and Debt

Having a bankruptcy or significant debt is not an automatic disqualification, but you may be asked to provide additional documentation to prove your financial responsibility.

Professional Conduct

Ethics and Integrity

The New Jersey Real Estate Commission places a strong emphasis on ethical behavior and integrity. Any history of unethical conduct, even if not directly related to real estate, could impact your eligibility.

Previous Licenses

If you have held a real estate license in another state, you must be in good standing with that state's real estate commission. Any disciplinary actions could affect your eligibility in New Jersey.

Application Process

Application Form

Once you meet all the eligibility criteria, the next step is to fill out the application form provided by the New Jersey Real Estate Commission. This form will ask for details about your education, background, and other qualifications.

Fees

There is an application fee that you must pay when submitting your application. The fee amount can vary, so it's advisable to check the latest information on the Commission's website.

Conclusion

Meeting the eligibility criteria is the first crucial step in your journey to becoming a licensed real estate agent in New Jersey. From age and education to legal status and professional conduct, each criterion serves to ensure that you are well-prepared for a career in this dynamic industry. Understanding these requirements in-depth will not only help you navigate the application process more smoothly but also set the foundation for a successful and ethical career in real estate. Therefore, take the time to familiarize yourself with each of these criteria and prepare accordingly to ensure that you meet them all.

Application Process

The application process for obtaining a real estate license in New Jersey is a comprehensive procedure that requires careful attention to detail. This chapter aims to guide you through each step, from initial preparations to the final submission of your application. We'll cover the documentation you'll need, the fees involved, and what to expect during the background checks and interviews. Let's dive in.

Initial Preparations

Research and Planning

Before you begin the application process, it's crucial to understand the New Jersey Real Estate Commission's requirements. This includes knowing the eligibility criteria, which we discussed in the previous chapter, and the specific documents you'll need to submit.

Pre-Licensing Education

Completing your pre-licensing education is a prerequisite for the application. Make sure you enroll in a school approved by the New Jersey Real Estate Commission and complete the required 75 hours of coursework. After completion, you'll receive a certificate, which you'll need to submit with your application.

Gathering Required Documents

Identification Documents

You'll need to provide valid identification, such as a driver's license or passport, to prove your age and citizenship status. Photocopies are generally not accepted, so be prepared to show the original documents.

Educational Certificates

Include your high school diploma or GED certificate along with your pre-licensing education certificate. These documents prove that you meet the educational requirements.

Legal Documents

If you're not a U.S. citizen, you'll need to provide proof of legal residency, such as a Green Card. Additionally, if your name has changed due to marriage or other reasons, legal documentation of the name change is required.

Completing the Application Form

Personal Information

The application form will ask for basic personal information, including your full name, address, and Social Security number. Make sure all the information is accurate to avoid delays.

Employment History

You'll be required to provide details about your employment history for the past five years. This includes the names and addresses of employers, your job titles, and the dates of employment.

Criminal History

If you have a criminal history, you'll need to provide details. Failure to disclose this information can result in disqualification. You'll also need to submit to a background check, which we'll discuss in more detail later.

Application Fee

There is a non-refundable application fee that you must pay when submitting your application. The fee can vary, so check the New Jersey Real Estate Commission's website for the most current information.

Background Check and Fingerprinting

Scheduling and Procedure

Once your application is received and initially reviewed, you'll be instructed to undergo a background check. This involves fingerprinting, which can be scheduled through approved service providers.

What They Look For

The background check will look for criminal history, financial stability, and any disciplinary actions from other professional licenses you may have held. It's a comprehensive review to ensure you meet the ethical and professional standards required for a real estate license.

Interview and Additional Documentation

Possible Interview

In some cases, you may be called for an interview with a representative from the New Jersey Real Estate Commission. This is generally to clarify any issues or questions they may have regarding your application.

Additional Documentation

If there are any discrepancies or issues with your application, you may be asked to provide additional documentation. This could include court records, financial statements, or further proof of employment or education.

Application Review and Approval

Timeframe

Once all documents are submitted, and the background check is complete, the Commission will review your application. This can take several weeks, so patience is key.

Notification

You'll be notified via mail or email about the status of your application. If approved, you'll receive instructions on scheduling your licensing exam. If denied, you'll be provided with reasons and information on how to appeal.

Conclusion

The application process for a real estate license in New Jersey is thorough and requires a meticulous approach. From gathering documents to undergoing background checks and possibly interviews, each step is designed to ensure that you're well-qualified and prepared for a career in real estate. By understanding what's required at each stage, you can navigate the process more smoothly and increase your chances of approval. Keep in mind that the New Jersey Real Estate Commission is your primary resource for the most current and accurate information, so don't hesitate to reach out to them with any questions or concerns.

Exam Format

The real estate licensing exam is a pivotal moment in your journey to becoming a real estate agent in New Jersey. This chapter aims to provide you with a comprehensive understanding of the exam format, the types of questions you'll encounter, and the strategies you can employ to maximize your chances of passing. By the end of this chapter, you'll have a solid grasp of what to expect and how to prepare effectively.

Structure of the Exam

Sections and Questions

The New Jersey Real Estate Licensing Exam is divided into two main sections: the National portion and the State-specific portion. The National portion typically consists of 80 multiple-choice questions, while the State-specific portion has around 50. You'll have a total of 4 hours to complete both sections.

Scoring

Each question carries equal weight, and there's no penalty for guessing. You'll need to score at least 70% on each section to pass. Your results are usually available immediately after completing the exam, and you'll receive a detailed score report.

Types of Questions

Recall Questions

These questions test your ability to remember facts and figures. For example, you might be asked to recall the number of days within which a buyer has the right to cancel a contract.

Application Questions

These questions require you to apply your knowledge to specific scenarios. For instance, you might be given a situation where a buyer and seller are in dispute and asked what steps should be taken according to New Jersey law.

Analysis Questions

These are the most complex types of questions. They require you to analyze different pieces of information and make judgments based on that analysis. For example, you might be given a set of financial statements for a property and asked to calculate its profitability.

Key Topics Covered

National Portion

- Property Ownership
- Land Use Controls and Regulations
- Valuation and Market Analysis
- Financing
- General Principles of Agency
- Property Disclosures

State-Specific Portion

- New Jersey Real Estate Commission Rules and Regulations
- Licensing Requirements
- State-specific Contract Laws
- Ethical and Legal Considerations in New Jersey

Strategies for Success

Time Management

With 4 hours to answer approximately 130 questions, you have roughly 1.8 minutes per question. Practice pacing yourself so that you have enough time to answer every question.

Elimination Technique

If you're unsure about an answer, try to eliminate the obviously incorrect choices first. This increases your odds if you have to guess.

Flagging for Review

Most exam software allows you to flag questions for review. If you're unsure about a question, flag it and move on. Return to it later if time permits.

Preparing for the Exam

Study Material

Utilize the study materials provided by your pre-licensing course, but also consider purchasing additional study guides and practice exams. The more diverse your study materials, the better prepared you'll be.

Practice Exams

Take as many practice exams as you can. This will not only familiarize you with the types of questions you'll encounter but also improve your time management skills.

Study Groups

Consider forming or joining a study group. Explaining concepts to peers can enhance your understanding, and you can gain from their insights.

Day Before the Exam

Review and Rest

Spend some time reviewing key concepts, but don't cram. Make sure to get a good night's sleep so you're well-rested for the exam.

Logistics

Make sure you know the exam location and how to get there. Plan to arrive early to account for any unexpected delays.

Day of the Exam

What to Bring

You'll need to bring a valid form of identification and any other materials specified by the testing center. Usually, calculators are provided, but check in advance to be sure.

During the Exam

Read each question carefully and don't rush. Use all the time allotted to you, and review your answers if time permits.

Conclusion

Understanding the format of the New Jersey Real Estate Licensing Exam is crucial for effective preparation and ultimately, for passing the exam. From the types of questions to expect to strategies for success, this chapter has aimed to provide a comprehensive guide to help you navigate this critical step in your real estate career. Remember, preparation is key, so make use of all available resources and give yourself ample time to study. Good luck!

Property Ownership and Land Use Controls

The real estate landscape in New Jersey is a complex web of laws, regulations, and practices that govern property ownership and land use. As a prospective real estate agent, understanding these intricacies is not just beneficial—it's essential. This chapter aims to provide a comprehensive guide to the types of property ownership, legal frameworks, and land use controls that are specific to New Jersey.

Types of Property Ownership

Fee Simple Absolute

In a Fee Simple Absolute, the owner has complete control over the property, including the land and any structures on it. This is the most straightforward type of ownership but is subject to federal and state laws.

Advantages: Full control, easy to transfer, can be mortgaged.
Disadvantages: Subject to taxation and can be foreclosed if mortgage payments are not made.

Life Estate

A life estate is a more complex form of ownership where the property is owned for the duration of someone's life, often the owner. After their death, the property reverts to a designated beneficiary.

Advantages: Beneficial for estate planning, can ensure family retains property.
Disadvantages: Difficult to sell or mortgage, limited control.

Leasehold Estate

In a Leasehold Estate, an individual or entity holds the right to occupy a property for a predetermined period, often in exchange for rent.

Advantages: Lower upfront costs, less responsibility for maintenance.
Disadvantages: No ownership equity, subject to the terms of a lease.

Joint Tenancy and Tenancy in Common

In Joint Tenancy, each owner has an equal share of the property. In Tenancy in Common, each owner can have a different percentage of ownership.

Advantages: Easier to manage, potential for income through renting.
Disadvantages: Conflicts can arise in joint decisions like selling the property.

Legal Frameworks Governing Property Ownership

Deeds

A deed is a legal document that signifies property ownership. In New Jersey, deeds must be recorded in the county where the property is located.

Warranty Deed: Guarantees that the seller owns the property free and clear.
Quitclaim Deed: Transfers any ownership the seller has but makes no guarantees.

Title Insurance

Title insurance protects against defects in the title and is usually required by mortgage lenders. It's crucial to understand the different types of title insurance policies available in New Jersey.

Easements

Easements give someone the right to use part of your land for a specific purpose. Utility companies often have easements for maintenance or emergency repair work.

Prescriptive Easement: Acquired through regular use.
Easement by Necessity: Created when a property is landlocked.

Covenants and Restrictions

Covenants are private agreements or contracts that dictate how a property can be used. They can be simple or complex and may include things like architectural guidelines or what types of businesses can operate on a property.

Land Use Controls and Regulations

Zoning Laws

Zoning laws in New Jersey can be complex due to the state's diverse range of urban, suburban, and rural areas. These laws can affect property taxes, school districts, and even your daily commute.

Residential Zones: Usually divided into categories like single-family, multi-family, etc.
Commercial Zones: These can include retail, office space, and other business types.
Industrial Zones: Usually reserved for manufacturing or other heavy industrial use.

Building Codes and Permits

Building codes set the minimum standards for construction and are enforced by local municipalities. Always check whether you need a permit for renovations or new construction.

Environmental Regulations

New Jersey has stringent environmental regulations, especially concerning water quality and wetlands. Violating these can result in hefty fines.

New Jersey-Specific Land Use Controls

Farmland Assessment Act

This act provides for lower property tax assessments on farmland.

Coastal Area Facility Review Act (CAFRA)

CAFRA permits are required for any development along the New Jersey coastline.

New Jersey Meadowlands Commission

This commission oversees land use in the Hackensack Meadowlands District, balancing environmental concerns with the needs of local communities.

Conclusion

Understanding property ownership and land use controls in New Jersey is a monumental task that requires continuous learning and adaptation. However, the rewards for mastering these subjects are equally significant, offering real estate professionals a competitive edge in a challenging market. This chapter has aimed to provide a thorough grounding in these topics, from the intricacies of deeds and titles to the complexities of zoning laws and environmental regulations. As you move forward in your real estate career, this knowledge will be invaluable, not only helping you pass your licensing exam but also preparing you for the practical challenges that lie ahead.

Mock Exam Property Ownership and Land Use Controls

➡1. What is the most complete form of ownership?

   A. Life Estate

   B. Leasehold Estate

   C. Fee Simple Absolute

   D. Joint Tenancy

   Answer: C. Fee Simple Absolute

   Fee Simple Absolute grants the owner all rights to the property, including the ability to sell, lease, or will it to heirs.

➡2. What does a life estate provide?

   A. Complete control of the property

   B. Ownership for the duration of someone's life

   C. Equal ownership among spouses

   D. Ownership for a specified period

   Answer: B. Ownership for the duration of someone's life

   A life estate grants ownership for the duration of someone's life, usually the life tenant. Upon their death, the property reverts to the original owner or a designated remainderman.

➡3. What is the primary advantage of a Leasehold Estate?

   A. Equity build-up

   B. Lower upfront costs

   C. Complete control

   D. Right of survivorship

Answer: B. Lower upfront costs

The primary advantage of a Leasehold Estate is lower upfront costs. The tenant has the right to occupy and use the property for a specified period, but ownership remains with the landlord.

➡4. What is unique about Joint Tenancy?

A. Unequal shares

B. No right of survivorship

C. Equal shares and right of survivorship

D. Complete control of the property

Answer: C. Equal shares and right of survivorship

Joint tenancy involves two or more people owning property with equal shares and the right of survivorship.

➡5. In which states is Community Property a common form of ownership?

A. All states

B. Only in community property states

C. Only in common law states

D. None of the above

Answer: B. Only in community property states

Community Property is a form of ownership common in community property states, where any property acquired during a marriage is considered jointly owned by both spouses.

➡6. What is the primary purpose of zoning laws?

A. To control property taxes

B. To regulate land use

C. To establish school districts

D. To determine property value

Answer: B. To regulate land use

Zoning laws are enacted by local governments to regulate how land can be used in specific areas.

➡**7. What is eminent domain?**

A. The right to lease property

B. The right of the government to take private property for public use

C. The right to inherit property

D. The right to sell property

Answer: B. The right of the government to take private property for public use

Eminent domain is the power of the government to take private property for public use, usually with compensation to the owner.

➡**8. What is a variance in the context of land use?**

A. A change in property value

B. A change in zoning laws

C. Permission to use land in a way that is prohibited by zoning laws

D. A change in property taxes

Answer: C. Permission to use land in a way that is prohibited by zoning laws

A variance is special permission granted by a zoning authority to use land in a manner that is generally not allowed under current zoning laws.

➡**9. What is a restrictive covenant?**

A. A government-imposed restriction on land use

B. A privately imposed agreement that restricts the use of land

C. A restriction on the sale of property

D. A restriction on leasing property

Answer: B. A privately imposed agreement that restricts the use of land

A restrictive covenant is an agreement that limits how a property owner can use their property, usually to preserve the value and integrity of a neighborhood.

➡10. What is the difference between real property and personal property?

A. Real property can be moved, but personal property cannot

B. Real property is land and anything permanently attached to it, while personal property is movable

C. Real property is always more valuable

D. There is no difference

Answer: B. Real property is land and anything permanently attached to it, while personal property is movable

Real property refers to land and anything permanently attached to it, like buildings. Personal property refers to movable items like furniture and cars.

➡11. What is a buffer zone in land use planning?

A. An area between residential and commercial zones

B. An area reserved for parks

C. An area where any type of construction is allowed

D. An area reserved for schools

Answer: A. An area between residential and commercial zones

A buffer zone is an area that separates different types of land uses, like residential and commercial, to reduce conflict between them.

➡12. What is the main goal of sustainable development?

A. To maximize profits

B. To use resources in a way that meets current needs without compromising future needs

C. To develop as quickly as possible

D. To use all available land

Answer: B. To use resources in a way that meets current needs without compromising future needs

Sustainable development aims to meet the needs of the present without compromising the ability of future generations to meet their own needs.

➡13. What is a master plan in the context of city planning?

A. A detailed budget

B. A long-term planning document that guides future growth and development

C. A short-term plan for immediate construction

D. A plan for a single building

Answer: B. A long-term planning document that guides future growth and development

A master plan is a comprehensive long-term plan that outlines the vision, policies, and goals for future growth and development in a city or community.

➡14. What is the main purpose of a building permit?

A. To raise revenue for the city

B. To ensure that construction complies with local codes and ordinances

C. To limit the number of buildings in an area

D. To increase property values

Answer: B. To ensure that construction complies with local codes and ordinances

A building permit is required to ensure that any new construction or significant changes to existing structures comply with local building codes and regulations.

➡15. What is the role of a property appraiser in land use?

A. To determine the highest and best use of a property

B. To enforce zoning laws

C. To issue building permits

D. To draft master plans

Answer: A. To determine the highest and best use of a property

A property appraiser assesses the value of a property based on its highest and best use, considering factors like location, zoning, and market conditions.

➡16. What is the "Right to Farm" law?

A. A law that allows anyone to farm anywhere

B. A law that protects farmers from nuisance lawsuits

C. A law that restricts farming to certain zones

D. A law that bans farming in urban areas

Answer: B. A law that protects farmers from nuisance lawsuits

The "Right to Farm" law is designed to protect existing farmers from nuisance lawsuits filed by new neighbors who may not be accustomed to the operations of a farm.

➡17. What does the term "infill development" refer to?

A. Developing farmland into residential areas

B. Developing open spaces in urban areas

C. Developing new structures on vacant or underused land within existing city boundaries

D. Expanding urban areas into rural zones

Answer: C. Developing new structures on vacant or underused land within existing city boundaries

Infill development aims to make use of vacant or underutilized lands within a built-up area for further construction or development.

➡**18. What is a nonconforming use?**

A. A use that conforms to current zoning laws but not to building codes

B. A use that was lawful before a zoning ordinance was passed but is no longer permitted

C. A use that violates both zoning laws and building codes

D. A use that is temporarily permitted due to a variance

Answer: B. A use that was lawful before a zoning ordinance was passed but is no longer permitted

A nonconforming use is a land use that was legal when established but does not conform to new or changed zoning laws.

➡**19. What is the main purpose of a land trust?**

A. To hold land for development

B. To preserve land for future generations

C. To generate revenue through land sales

D. To control land prices

Answer: B. To preserve land for future generations

A land trust is an organization that actively works to conserve land by undertaking or assisting in land or conservation easement acquisition.

➡**20. What is "mixed-use development"?**

A. Development that includes both residential and commercial properties

B. Development that is used for industrial purposes

C. Development that is only used for residential purposes

D. Development that is only used for commercial purposes

Answer: A. Development that includes both residential and commercial properties

Mixed-use development is a type of urban development that blends residential, commercial, cultural, institutional, or entertainment uses.

➡**21. What is the primary purpose of a greenbelt?**

A. To provide recreational spaces

B. To separate urban areas from rural areas

C. To increase property values

D. To reduce air pollution

Answer: B. To separate urban areas from rural areas

A greenbelt is an area of largely undeveloped, wild, or agricultural land surrounding or neighboring urban areas.

➡**22. What is "brownfield land"?**

A. Land that is used for agricultural purposes

B. Land that has been contaminated by hazardous waste

C. Land that is reserved for parks and recreation

D. Land that is zoned for industrial use

Answer: B. Land that has been contaminated by hazardous waste

Brownfield land is a term used in urban planning to describe any previously developed land that is not currently in use and may be potentially contaminated.

➡**23. What does "highest and best use" mean in the context of real estate?**

A. The use that generates the most income

B. The use that is most suitable from a social perspective

C. The use that maximizes a property's value

D. The use that is most environmentally sustainable

Answer: C. The use that maximizes a property's value

"Highest and best use" is a real estate appraisal term for the most profitable, likely use of a property, which is physically possible, appropriately supported, and legally permissible.

➥**24. What is "air rights"?**

A. The right to unlimited views from a property

B. The right to the air above the land

C. The right to pollute the air

D. The right to fresh air

Answer: B. The right to the air above the land

Air rights are a type of development right in real estate, referring to the empty space above a property.

➥**25. What is "land banking"?**

A. The process of buying land as an investment

B. The process of rezoning land

C. The process of converting agricultural land to residential land

D. The process of accumulating land for future development

Answer: D. The process of accumulating land for future development

Land banking is the practice of aggregating parcels of land for future sale or development.

➥**26. What is "eminent domain"?**

A. The right of the government to tax property

B. The right of the government to seize private property for public use

C. The right of the property owner to change the zoning laws

D. The right of the property owner to deny access to government officials

Answer: B. The right of the government to seize private property for public use

Eminent domain is the power of the government to take private property and convert it into public use, often with compensation to the owner.

➡**27. What is "spot zoning"?**

A. Zoning that changes frequently

B. Zoning that applies to a specific area within a larger zoned area

C. Zoning that applies only to commercial properties

D. Zoning that applies only during certain times of the year

Answer: B. Zoning that applies to a specific area within a larger zoned area

Spot zoning is the application of zoning laws that are different from the surrounding area, usually benefiting a single property owner.

➡**28. What does "buffer zone" mean in the context of land use?**

A. An area that separates different types of land uses

B. An area that is restricted for military use

C. An area that is designated for future development

D. An area that is kept empty for aesthetic purposes

Answer: A. An area that separates different types of land uses

A buffer zone is a zonal area that lies between two or more other areas that are contrasting in nature.

➡**29. What is "downzoning"?**

A. Changing the zoning of a property to a less intensive use

B. Changing the zoning of a property to a more intensive use

C. Rezoning to allow for higher buildings

D. Rezoning to allow for commercial use

Answer: A. Changing the zoning of a property to a less intensive use

Downzoning is the rezoning of land to a more restrictive zone to prevent overdevelopment.

➡ **30. What is "land grading"?**

A. The process of making land more level

B. The process of evaluating the quality of soil

C. The process of determining the value of the land

D. The process of rezoning land

Answer: A. The process of making land more level

Land grading is the act of leveling the surface of the soil to prepare it for construction or agriculture.

➡ **31. What is "land reclamation"?**

A. The process of converting developed land back to its natural state

B. The process of converting barren land into arable land

C. The process of restoring contaminated land

D. All of the above

Answer: D. All of the above

Land reclamation can involve converting barren land into arable land, restoring contaminated land, or converting developed land back to its natural state.

➡ **32. What is "land tenure"?**

A. The legal regime in which land is owned

B. The length of time land has been owned by a single entity

C. The tax status of a piece of land

D. The zoning classification of a piece of land

Answer: A. The legal regime in which land is owned

Land tenure is the way land is held or owned at the individual or collective level.

➡**33. What is "land partition"?**

A. The division of a larger piece of land into smaller lots

B. The legal process to settle land disputes

C. The change of land zoning types

D. The process of land reclamation

Answer: A. The division of a larger piece of land into smaller lots

Land partition is the division of real property into two or more parcels.

➡**34. What is "land speculation"?**

A. Buying land with the hope that its value will increase

B. Buying land for immediate development

C. Buying land for long-term investment

D. Buying land for agricultural use

Answer: A. Buying land with the hope that its value will increase

Land speculation is the purchase of land with the hope that it will increase in value for resale at a profit.

➡**35. What is "land surveying"?**

A. The process of measuring land and its features

B. The process of evaluating the quality of soil

C. The process of determining the value of the land

D. The process of rezoning land

Answer: A. The process of measuring land and its features

Land surveying is the technique of determining the terrestrial or three-dimensional position of points and the distances and angles between them.

→**36. What is "inclusionary zoning"?**

A. Zoning that includes only residential properties

B. Zoning that mandates a portion of new development be affordable for low-income households

C. Zoning that includes only commercial properties

D. Zoning that includes only industrial properties

Answer: B. Zoning that mandates a portion of new development be affordable for low-income households

Inclusionary zoning is a regulation that requires a given share of new construction to be affordable for people with low to moderate incomes.

→**37. What is "land banking"?**

A. The process of buying land for immediate development

B. The process of holding onto land as a long-term investment

C. The process of using land as collateral for a loan

D. The process of converting barren land into arable land

Answer: B. The process of holding onto land as a long-term investment

Land banking is the practice of aggregating parcels of land for future sale or development.

→**38. What does "air rights" refer to?**

A. The right to unlimited height in building above a property

B. The right to clean air in a residential area

C. The right to the airspace above the physical property

D. The right to fly drones over a property

Answer: C. The right to the airspace above the physical property

Air rights are the property interest in the "space" above the earth's surface.

➡ **39. What is "land assembly"?**

A. The process of gathering various small parcels of land into a single larger parcel

B. The process of constructing a building on a piece of land

C. The process of converting barren land into arable land

D. The process of dividing a larger piece of land into smaller lots

Answer: A. The process of gathering various small parcels of land into a single larger parcel

Land assembly is the process by which smaller parcels of land are combined to create a single larger parcel.

➡ **40. What is "land degradation"?**

A. The process of land losing its productivity due to human activities

B. The process of land increasing in value

C. The process of land being rezoned for less intensive use

D. The process of land being converted into a natural reserve

Answer: A. The process of land losing its productivity due to human activities

Land degradation refers to the deterioration or loss of the productive capacity of the soils for present and future.

➡ **41. What is "land improvement"?**

A. The process of adding value to a land through developments like roads and utilities

B. The process of converting barren land into arable land

C. The process of rezoning land for more intensive use

D. The process of restoring contaminated land

Answer: A. The process of adding value to a land through developments like roads and utilities

Land improvement refers to the effort made to make land more usable and valuable.

➡**42. What is "land lease"?**

A. A contract where the landowner gives another the right to use land in exchange for rent

B. A contract to sell land

C. A contract to buy land

D. A contract to develop land

Answer: A. A contract where the landowner gives another the right to use land in exchange for rent

A land lease is an agreement where the landowner permits a tenant to use the land in exchange for rent.

➡**43. What is "land reservation"?**

A. Land set aside for future use

B. Land set aside for indigenous people

C. Land set aside for environmental protection

D. All of the above

Answer: D. All of the above

Land reservation can refer to land set aside for various purposes, including future use, protection of indigenous rights, or environmental conservation.

➡44. What is "land trust"?

A. A legal entity that holds the ownership of a land for the benefit of another party

B. A company that invests in land

C. A non-profit organization that protects land for future generations

D. A government agency that manages public lands

Answer: A. A legal entity that holds the ownership of a land for the benefit of another party

A land trust is a legal entity that takes ownership of, or authority over, a property at the behest of the property owner.

➡45. What is "land use planning"?

A. The process of managing land resources to prevent land degradation

B. The process of determining the best way to use land resources

C. The process of rezoning land

D. The process of converting barren land into arable land

Answer: B. The process of determining the best way to use land resources

Land use planning involves the systematic assessment of land and water potential, alternatives for land use, and the economic and social conditions.

➡46. What does "eminent domain" refer to?

A. The right of the government to take private property for public use

B. The right of a landlord to evict a tenant for non-payment of rent

C. The right of a property owner to develop their land as they see fit

D. The right of a tenant to enjoy their rented property without interference from the landlord

Answer: A. The right of the government to take private property for public use

Eminent domain is the power of the government to take private property and convert it into public use, usually with compensation to the owner.

➡47. What is "adverse possession"?

A. The illegal occupation of property

B. The acquisition of property through inheritance

C. The acquisition of property through a long-term, open, and notorious occupation

D. The acquisition of property through a legal purchase

Answer: C. The acquisition of property through a long-term, open, and notorious occupation

Adverse possession is a legal principle that allows a person who possesses someone else's land for an extended period of time to claim legal title to that land.

➡48. What is "land value tax"?

A. A tax on the value of a building

B. A tax on the value of land, excluding the value of buildings and improvements

C. A tax on the sale of land

D. A tax on the rental income from land

Answer: B. A tax on the value of land, excluding the value of buildings and improvements
A land value tax is a levy on the unimproved value of land.

➡49. What is "landlocked property"?

A. Property that is surrounded by other properties, with no direct access to a public road

B. Property that is located far from any body of water

C. Property that is not subject to flooding

D. Property that is restricted from development

Answer: A. Property that is surrounded by other properties, with no direct access to a public road

Landlocked property is real estate that has no direct access to a public street, so you can't get to it unless you go through someone else's property first.

→ 50. What is "latent defect"?

A. A defect that is obvious and easy to spot

B. A defect that is hidden and not immediately obvious

C. A defect that has been disclosed by the seller

D. A defect that has been repaired before the sale of the property

Answer: B. A defect that is hidden and not immediately obvious

A latent defect is a fault in the property that could not have been discovered by a reasonably thorough inspection before the sale.

Laws of Agency and Fiduciary Duties

Understanding the laws of agency and fiduciary duties is crucial for anyone aspiring to be a successful real estate agent in New Jersey. These laws and duties define the relationship between the agent and the client, setting the ethical and legal standards that must be adhered to. This chapter aims to provide an in-depth look into these important aspects of real estate practice in New Jersey.

The Concept of Agency

Definition

Agency in real estate refers to the relationship between the real estate agent and the client. The agent represents the client in property transactions, acting on their behalf.

Types of Agency Relationships

Seller's Agent: Represents the seller and owes fiduciary duties to the seller.

Buyer's Agent: Represents the buyer and owes fiduciary duties to the buyer.

Dual Agent: Represents both the buyer and the seller in the same transaction.

Sub-agent: Works under another agent but represents the client of the supervising agent.

Fiduciary Duties

Definition

Fiduciary duties are the responsibilities that an agent owes to their client. These duties are often summarized by the acronym "OLD CAR," which stands for Obedience, Loyalty, Disclosure, Confidentiality, Accountability, and Reasonable Care.

Obedience

The agent must obey all lawful instructions from their client, as long as these instructions are within the scope of the agency agreement.

Loyalty

The agent must put the client's interests above all others, including their own. This means avoiding conflicts of interest and always acting in the best interests of the client.

Disclosure

The agent is required to disclose all material facts that could affect the client's decision-making process. This includes any conflicts of interest the agent may have.

Confidentiality

The agent must keep all client information confidential unless required by law to disclose it or if the client gives permission.

Accountability

The agent is responsible for keeping track of all funds and property related to the transaction.

Reasonable Care

The agent must exercise reasonable care and diligence when performing their duties, including staying informed about market conditions and relevant laws.

New Jersey-Specific Laws and Regulations

New Jersey Real Estate Commission (NJREC)

The NJREC is responsible for licensing real estate agents in New Jersey and ensuring that they comply with state laws and regulations.

Disclosure Requirements

In New Jersey, agents are required to provide a Consumer Information Statement (CIS) to all buyers and sellers. This document outlines the types of agency relationships and the duties owed in each.

Dual Agency

Dual agency is legal in New Jersey but must be disclosed and agreed upon in writing by all parties involved.

Termination of Agency

In New Jersey, the agency relationship can be terminated by mutual agreement, expiration of the agency agreement, or completion of the transaction.

Ethical Considerations

Code of Ethics

Many real estate agents in New Jersey are members of the National Association of Realtors (NAR), which has its own Code of Ethics. This code provides additional guidelines on how agents should conduct themselves.

Ethical Dilemmas

Agents may face ethical dilemmas, such as whether to represent friends or family, how to handle multiple offers, or what to do if they have inside information about a property.

Legal Consequences of Breach of Duty

Failure to adhere to fiduciary duties or state laws can result in various penalties, including fines, license suspension or revocation, and even legal action from the client.

Conclusion

Understanding the laws of agency and fiduciary duties is not just a requirement for passing the New Jersey Real Estate License Exam; it's essential for a successful career. These laws and duties serve as the foundation for all interactions between agents and clients, ensuring that transactions are conducted ethically and legally. By adhering to these guidelines, you not only protect your clients but also yourself, making you a more trustworthy and reliable real estate agent.

Mock Exam Laws of Agency and Fiduciary Duties

➡1. What is the primary role of an agent in a real estate transaction?

A. To represent the buyer only

B. To act on behalf of the principal

C. To market the property

D. To negotiate the best price for themselves

Answer: B

The primary role of an agent is to act on behalf of the principal, whether that's the buyer or the seller.

➡2. Which of the following is NOT a fiduciary duty an agent owes to their client?

A. Loyalty

B. Disclosure

C. Profit maximization

D. Confidentiality

Answer: C

Profit maximization is not a fiduciary duty. The fiduciary duties include loyalty, disclosure, and confidentiality among others.

➡3. What is dual agency?

A. When two agents represent a buyer

B. When an agent represents both buyer and seller

C. When two agents represent a seller

D. When an agent represents two buyers

Answer: B

Dual agency occurs when an agent represents both the buyer and the seller in a single transaction.

➡4. Which state law is most likely to govern real estate agency relationships?

A. Federal law

B. Common law

C. State-specific law

D. International law

Answer: C

Each state has its own set of laws and regulations governing real estate agency relationships.

➡5. What must an agent do if they are involved in a dual agency situation?

A. Keep it a secret

B. Get written consent from both parties

C. Represent the buyer's interests only

D. Represent the seller's interests only

Answer: B

In a dual agency situation, both parties must be made fully aware of the dual agency and consent to it in writing.

➡6. What does the fiduciary duty of "reasonable care and skill" entail?

A. Making the most money for the client

B. Acting as any competent agent would

C. Keeping all information confidential

D. Always being available for the client

Answer: B

The duty of "reasonable care and skill" means the agent must act as any competent agent would in the same situation.

→7. **What is the primary focus of the fiduciary duty of "loyalty"?**

A. Maximizing profit for the agent

B. Putting the client's needs above the agent's

C. Keeping all information confidential

D. Disclosing all facts to the client

Answer: B

The fiduciary duty of "loyalty" requires the agent to always act in the best interest of their client.

→8. **What is the consequence of breaching fiduciary duties?**

A. Loss of job

B. Legal liabilities

C. A warning

D. No consequences

Answer: B

Breaching fiduciary duties can result in various legal liabilities, including fines and loss of license.

→9. **What is the purpose of an agency agreement?**

A. To outline the agent's commission

B. To outline the scope of the agent's responsibilities

C. To protect the agent from legal action

D. To list the properties for sale

Answer: B

An agency agreement outlines the scope of the agent's responsibilities and how they will be compensated.

➡10. Which of the following is NOT a type of agency relationship in real estate?

A. Seller's agent

B. Buyer's agent

C. Independent agent

D. Dual agent

Answer: C

"Independent agent" is not a standard type of agency relationship in real estate. The common types are seller's agent, buyer's agent, and dual agent.

➡11. What is the term for the person represented by an agent?

A. Client

B. Customer

C. Broker

D. Associate

Answer: A

The person represented by an agent is referred to as the client.

➡12. What is the fiduciary duty of "disclosure" primarily concerned with?

A. Revealing all known facts that materially affect the property

B. Keeping the client's information confidential

C. Making the most money for the client

D. Always being available for the client

Answer: A

The fiduciary duty of "disclosure" requires the agent to reveal all known facts that materially affect the property's value.

➡13. What is the opposite of a dual agency?

A. Single agency

B. Triple agency

C. No agency

D. Sub-agency

Answer: A

The opposite of a dual agency is a single agency, where the agent represents only one party in the transaction.

➡14. What is the primary purpose of a buyer's agent?

A. To represent the seller

B. To represent the buyer

C. To market the property

D. To negotiate the best price for themselves

Answer: B

The primary purpose of a buyer's agent is to represent the buyer's interests in the transaction.

➡15. What is the fiduciary duty of "obedience" concerned with?

A. Following all of the client's lawful instructions

B. Disclosing all material facts

C. Keeping all information confidential

D. Making the most money for the client

Answer: A

The fiduciary duty of "obedience" requires the agent to follow all lawful instructions from their client.

➡16. What is the primary role of a sub-agent?

A. To represent the buyer

B. To represent the seller

C. To assist the primary agent

D. To market the property

Answer: C

The primary role of a sub-agent is to assist the primary agent in fulfilling their duties.

➡17. What is the fiduciary duty of "accounting"?

A. Keeping track of all financial transactions

B. Disclosing all material facts

C. Keeping all information confidential

D. Making the most money for the client

Answer: A

The fiduciary duty of "accounting" requires the agent to keep track of all financial transactions related to the agency relationship.

➡18. What is the primary purpose of a listing agreement?

A. To outline the buyer's needs

B. To outline the scope of the agent's responsibilities towards the seller

C. To protect the agent from legal action

D. To list the properties for rent

Answer: B

A listing agreement outlines the scope of the agent's responsibilities towards the seller and how they will be compensated.

➡19. What is the term for an agent who represents the seller?

A. Buyer's agent

B. Seller's agent

C. Dual agent

D. Sub-agent

Answer: B

An agent who represents the seller is known as a seller's agent.

➡20. What is the consequence of not disclosing a dual agency?

A. Loss of job

B. Legal liabilities

C. A warning

D. No consequences

Answer: B

Failure to disclose a dual agency can result in legal liabilities, including fines and loss of license.

➡21. What is the primary role of a transaction broker?

A. To represent the buyer

B. To represent the seller

C. To facilitate the transaction without representing either party

D. To market the property

Answer: C

A transaction broker's primary role is to facilitate the real estate transaction without representing either the buyer or the seller.

➡22. What does the fiduciary duty of "loyalty" require?

A. Disclosing all material facts

B. Putting the client's interests above all others

C. Keeping all information confidential

D. Following all of the client's instructions

Answer: B

The fiduciary duty of "loyalty" requires the agent to put the client's interests above all others, including their own.

➡23. What is the term for an agent who represents both the buyer and the seller in the same transaction?

A. Single agent

D. Dual agent

C. Sub-agent

D. Transaction broker

Answer: B

An agent who represents both the buyer and the seller in the same transaction is known as a dual agent.

➡24. What is the fiduciary duty of "reasonable care and diligence" concerned with?

A. Protecting the client's financial interests

B. Disclosing all material facts

C. Keeping all information confidential

D. Following all of the client's instructions

Answer: A

The fiduciary duty of "reasonable care and diligence" requires the agent to protect the client's financial interests in the transaction.

25. What is the term for a written agreement between the agent and the client?

A. Listing agreement

B. Agency agreement

C. Contract

D. Memorandum of understanding

Answer: B

A written agreement between the agent and the client outlining the scope of their relationship is known as an agency agreement.

26. What is the primary purpose of a seller's agent?

A. To represent the buyer

B. To represent the seller

C. To market the property

D. To negotiate the best price for themselves

Answer: B

The primary purpose of a seller's agent is to represent the seller's interests in the transaction.

27. What is the fiduciary duty of "confidentiality" concerned with?

A. Protecting the client's financial interests

B. Disclosing all material facts

C. Keeping all information confidential

D. Following all of the client's instructions

Answer: C

The fiduciary duty of "confidentiality" requires the agent to keep all client information confidential unless required to disclose it by law.

➡28. What is the term for an agent who does not represent either party and simply facilitates the transaction?

A. Single agent

B. Dual agent

C. Transaction broker

D. Sub-agent

Answer: C

An agent who does not represent either party and simply facilitates the transaction is known as a transaction broker.

➡29. What is the primary purpose of a dual agent?

A. To represent the buyer

B. To represent the seller

C. To represent both the buyer and the seller

D. To market the property

Answer: C

The primary purpose of a dual agent is to represent both the buyer and the seller in the same transaction.

➡30. What is the fiduciary duty of "full disclosure" concerned with?

A. Protecting the client's financial interests

B. Disclosing all material facts

C. Keeping all information confidential

D. Following all of the client's instructions

Answer: B

The fiduciary duty of "full disclosure" requires the agent to disclose all material facts that could affect the client's decisions.

➡️**31. What is the term for an agent who represents the buyer exclusively?**

A. Buyer's agent

B. Seller's agent

C. Dual agent

D. Transaction broker

Answer: A

A buyer's agent exclusively represents the buyer's interests in a real estate transaction.

➡️**32. What is the term used to describe the agent's responsibility to act in the best interests of the client?**

A. Loyalty

B. Obedience

C. Disclosure

D. Confidentiality

Answer: A

The term "loyalty" is used to describe the agent's fiduciary duty to act in the best interests of the client.

➡33. What is the legal obligation called when an agent must keep the client's information confidential even after the agency relationship has ended?

    A. Perpetual confidentiality

    B. Eternal secrecy

    C. Ongoing disclosure

    D. Extended loyalty

Answer: A

The legal obligation is called "perpetual confidentiality," requiring the agent to keep the client's information confidential indefinitely, even after the agency relationship has ended.

➡34. What does the fiduciary duty of "accounting" require?

    A. Keeping accurate financial records

    B. Disclosing all material facts

    C. Keeping all information confidential

    D. Following all of the client's instructions

Answer: A

The fiduciary duty of "accounting" requires the agent to keep accurate financial records related to the transaction.

➡35. What is the term for a written agreement between a buyer and an agent?

    A. Buyer's agreement

    B. Listing agreement

    C. Agency agreement

    D. Purchase agreement

Answer: A

A written agreement between a buyer and an agent is known as a buyer's agreement.

➡36. What is the primary purpose of a listing agent?

A. To represent the buyer

B. To represent the seller

C. To market the property

D. To negotiate the best price for themselves

Answer: C

The primary purpose of a listing agent is to market the property to potential buyers.

➡37. What is the fiduciary duty of "disclosure" concerned with?

A. Protecting the client's financial interests

B. Disclosing all material facts

C. Keeping all information confidential

D. Following all of the client's instructions

Answer: B

The fiduciary duty of "disclosure" requires the agent to disclose all material facts that could affect the client's decisions.

➡38. What is the term for an agent who represents the seller exclusively?

A. Buyer's agent

B. Seller's agent

C. Dual agent

D. Transaction broker

Answer: B

A seller's agent exclusively represents the seller's interests in a real estate transaction.

➡39. What is the primary role of a dual agent?

A. To represent the buyer

B. To represent the seller

C. To represent both the buyer and the seller

D. To market the property

Answer: C

The primary role of a dual agent is to represent both the buyer and the seller in the same transaction.

➡40. What is the fiduciary duty of "loyalty" concerned with?

A. Protecting the client's financial interests

B. Disclosing all material facts

C. Keeping all information confidential

D. Putting the client's interests above all others

Answer: D

The fiduciary duty of "loyalty" requires the agent to put the client's interests above all others, including their own.

➡41. What is the primary purpose of a buyer's agent in a real estate transaction?

A. To represent the seller's interests

B. To represent the buyer's interests

C. To act as a neutral third party

D. To facilitate the transaction without representation

Answer: B

The primary purpose of a buyer's agent is to represent the interests of the buyer in a real estate transaction.

➥42. What is the fiduciary duty that requires an agent to be honest and forthright with the client?

   A. Loyalty

   B. Disclosure

   C. Obedience

   D. Accountability

Answer: B

The fiduciary duty of disclosure requires an agent to be honest and forthright with the client, providing all relevant information.

➥43. What is the term for the legal relationship between a principal and an agent where the agent is expected to represent the principal's interests?

   A. Contractual agreement

   B. Fiduciary relationship

   C. Business partnership

   D. Legal guardianship

Answer: B

The term "fiduciary relationship" describes the legal relationship between a principal and an agent, where the agent is expected to represent the principal's interests with the utmost good faith, trust, confidence, and candor.

➥44. What is the fiduciary duty that requires an agent to follow all lawful instructions from the client?

   A. Obedience

   B. Loyalty

   C. Disclosure

D. Accountability

Answer: A

The fiduciary duty of obedience requires an agent to follow all lawful instructions given by the client.

➡️**45. What is the term used to describe the agent's responsibility to safeguard the client's financial interests?**

A. Accountability
B. Loyalty
C. Disclosure
D. Obedience

Answer: A

The term "accountability" is used to describe the agent's fiduciary duty to safeguard the client's financial interests.

➡️**46. What is the legal obligation called when an agent must disclose any known defects of the property?**

A. Material fact disclosure
B. Defect revelation
C. Condition reporting
D. Property transparency

Answer: A

The legal obligation is called "material fact disclosure," requiring the agent to disclose any known defects of the property to the client.

→47. What is the term used to describe the agent's responsibility to keep the client informed at all times?

  A. Loyalty

  B. Disclosure

  C. Obedience

  D. Accountability

Answer: B

The term "disclosure" is used to describe the agent's fiduciary duty to keep the client informed at all times.

→48. In a dual agency relationship, what must the agent do to avoid conflicts of interest?

  A. Represent only the buyer's interests

  B. Represent only the seller's interests

  C. Obtain written consent from both parties

  D. Avoid disclosing any confidential information to either party

Answer: C

In a dual agency relationship, the agent must obtain written consent from both parties to avoid conflicts of interest. This ensures that both the buyer and the seller are aware of the situation and agree to it.

→49. Which of the following is NOT a duty of an agent towards their client?

  A. Confidentiality

  B. Obedience

  C. Disclosure

  D. Independence

Answer: D

Independence is not a duty of an agent towards their client. Agents are expected to act in the best interests of their clients, which includes duties like confidentiality, obedience, and disclosure.

➡50. What is the term for a situation where an agent represents both the buyer and the seller in a transaction?

   A. Double agency
   B. Single agency
   C. Sub-agency
   D. Non-agency

Answer: A

The term for a situation where an agent represents both the buyer and the seller in a transaction is called "double agency." This situation requires informed consent from both parties and can present a conflict of interest for the agent.

Property Valuation and Financial Analysis

Property valuation and financial analysis are critical components in the real estate industry, especially in a diverse and complex market like New Jersey. Whether you're a buyer, a seller, or an agent, understanding how properties are valued and how to analyze the financial aspects of a real estate transaction can make a significant difference in your success. This chapter will delve into the various methods of property valuation, key financial metrics, and New Jersey-specific considerations.

Property Valuation Methods

Comparative Market Analysis (CMA)

A Comparative Market Analysis is often the first step in property valuation. It involves comparing the property in question to similar properties that have recently sold, are currently on the market, or were listed but did not sell. Factors like location, size, and condition are considered.

Cost Approach

This method calculates the cost to build a similar property from scratch, considering the cost of land and construction materials. It's often used for new properties or unique homes where comparable sales are hard to find.

Income Approach

This approach is commonly used for rental properties. It involves calculating the Net Operating Income (NOI) and applying a capitalization rate to determine the property's value.

Key Financial Metrics

Return on Investment (ROI)

ROI measures the profitability of an investment property. It's calculated by dividing the net profit of the property by the initial investment cost.

Cash Flow

Cash flow is the net income generated by the property after all expenses have been deducted. Positive cash flow is a good indicator of a profitable investment.

Capitalization Rate (Cap Rate)

The cap rate is used to evaluate the potential return on an investment property. It's calculated by dividing the NOI by the current market value of the property.

New Jersey-Specific Considerations

Property Taxes

New Jersey has some of the highest property taxes in the country, which can significantly impact both valuation and financial analysis.

Rent Control Laws

Some areas in New Jersey have rent control laws, which can affect the income potential of rental properties.

Coastal Properties

The value of coastal properties can be significantly impacted by factors like proximity to the ocean, flood zones, and local regulations.

Financial Analysis Tools

Mortgage Calculators

These tools can help you determine your monthly payments, how much you can afford, and the impact of different interest rates.

Investment Property Analyzers

These are specialized software or online tools that can help you evaluate the financial metrics of an investment property.

Case Studies

Case Study 1: Single-Family Home in Newark

This case study will walk you through a CMA, considering factors like location, recent sales, and market trends.

Case Study 2: Multi-Family Property in Jersey City

This case study focuses on the income approach, considering rent control laws and property taxes.

Conclusion

Understanding property valuation and financial analysis is crucial for anyone involved in the New Jersey real estate market. These skills not only help in making informed decisions but also in negotiating better deals and maximizing returns. Whether you're preparing for the New Jersey Real Estate License Exam or looking to invest in the state's diverse property market, a solid grasp of these concepts is indispensable.

Mock Exam Property Valuation and Financial Analysis

➡1. Which property valuation method is most commonly used for residential properties?

    A. Sales Comparison Approach

    B. Cost Approach

    C. Income Approach

    D. ROI Method

Answer: A. Sales Comparison Approach

The Sales Comparison Approach is most commonly used for residential properties. It involves comparing the property to similar ones that have recently sold.

➡2. What does ROI stand for in real estate financial analysis?

    A. Return On Investment

    B. Rate Of Interest

    C. Real Estate Opportunity Index

    D. Return On Infrastructure

Answer: A. Return On Investment

ROI stands for Return On Investment. It's a key metric used to evaluate the profitability of an investment property.

➡3. What is the Debt Service Coverage Ratio (DSCR) used for?

    A. Calculating property taxes

    B. Assessing a property's ability to cover its debt obligations

    C. Determining the property's market value

    D. Calculating the monthly rent

Answer: B. Assessing a property's ability to cover its debt obligations

DSCR is used to assess a property's ability to cover its debt obligations. A DSCR greater than 1 indicates that the property is generating sufficient income to cover its debts.

➠4. Which of the following factors does NOT affect property valuation?

   A. Location

   B. Size and Layout

   C. Color of the walls

   D. Market Conditions

Answer: C. Color of the walls

The color of the walls is generally not a significant factor affecting property valuation. Location, size, and market conditions are more impactful.

➠5. What is Cash Flow Analysis used for in real estate?

   A. Calculating monthly income and expenses

   B. Assessing property taxes

   C. Determining market value

   D. Calculating ROI

Answer: A. Calculating monthly income and expenses

Cash Flow Analysis is used to calculate the monthly income generated by the property, subtracting all expenses, to determine the net cash flow.

➠6. What does a DSCR of less than 1 indicate?

   A. The property is generating sufficient income

   B. The property is not generating enough income to cover debts

   C. The property is overvalued

   D. The property is undervalued

Answer: B. The property is not generating enough income to cover debts**

A DSCR of less than 1 indicates that the property is not generating sufficient income to cover its debt obligations.

➡7. In the Sales Comparison Approach, what is adjusted for when comparing properties?

A. Only the size

B. Only the location

C. Features, location, and other factors

D. Only the features

Answer: C. Features, location, and other factors

Explanation: In the Sales Comparison Approach, adjustments are made for differences in features, location, and other factors to make a fair comparison.

➡8. What is the Cost Approach commonly used for?

A. Old properties

B. New properties

C. Commercial properties

D. Rental properties

Answer: B. New properties

Explanation: The Cost Approach is often used for new properties. It involves calculating how much it would cost to replace the property, then adjusting for depreciation and land value.

➡9. Which of the following is NOT a financial analysis tool in real estate?

A. ROI

B. DSCR

C. Cash Flow Analysis

D. Gross Domestic Product (GDP)

Answer: D. Gross Domestic Product (GDP)

GDP is not a financial analysis tool used in real estate. ROI, DSCR, and Cash Flow Analysis are commonly used metrics.

➡ **10. What is the Income Approach commonly used for?**

A. Residential properties

B. Commercial properties

C. New properties

D. Old properties

Answer: B. Commercial properties

The Income Approach is commonly used for commercial properties. It involves calculating the present value of future cash flows the property is expected to generate.

➡ **11. What does the term 'amortization' refer to in real estate?**

A. The process of increasing property value

B. The gradual reduction of a loan balance through regular payments

C. The increase in property tax over time

D. The depreciation of property value due to age

Answer: B. The gradual reduction of a loan balance through regular payments

Amortization refers to the gradual reduction of a loan balance through regular payments over time.

➡ **12. What is the primary focus of a Comparative Market Analysis (CMA)?**

A. To compare the ROI of different properties

B. To assess the fair market value of a property

C. To evaluate the debt service coverage ratio

D. To calculate the net operating income

Answer: B. To assess the fair market value of a property

A Comparative Market Analysis (CMA) is primarily used to assess the fair market value of a property by comparing it to similar properties that have recently sold or are currently on the market.

➡13. What does LTV stand for in real estate?

   A. Loan To Value

   B. Long Term Viability

   C. Lease To Vendor

   D. Land Transfer Value

Answer: A. Loan To Value

LTV stands for Loan To Value, which is a ratio that compares the amount of a loan to the value of the property being purchased.

➡14. What is the primary purpose of a cap rate in real estate?

   A. To measure the risk associated with a property

   B. To calculate the monthly mortgage payment

   C. To determine the property tax rate

   D. To assess the age of the property

Answer: A. To measure the risk associated with a property

The cap rate, or capitalization rate, is used to measure the risk associated with a property and its potential return on investment.

➡15. What is the formula for calculating Net Operating Income (NOI)?

A. Gross Income - Operating Expenses

B. Gross Income + Operating Expenses

C. (Gross Income - Operating Expenses) / Gross Income

D. Operating Expenses - Gross Income

Answer: A. Gross Income - Operating Expenses

Net Operating Income (NOI) is calculated by subtracting operating expenses from the gross income generated by the property.

➡16. What is the Debt Service Coverage Ratio (DSCR) primarily used for?

A. To determine the profitability of a property

B. To assess a borrower's ability to cover loan payments

C. To calculate property taxes

D. To evaluate the market value of a property

Answer: B. To assess a borrower's ability to cover loan payments

DSCR is used to evaluate a borrower's ability to cover loan payments from the property's net operating income.

➡17. What does the Gross Rent Multiplier (GRM) measure?

A. The property's operating expenses

B. The property's potential for appreciation

C. The property's value relative to its gross rental income

D. The property's maintenance costs

Answer: C. The property's value relative to its gross rental income

GRM measures the property's value in relation to its gross rental income.

➡18. What is the primary purpose of a 'due diligence' period in real estate transactions?

A. To secure financing

B. To conduct inspections and verify property details

C. To negotiate the price

D. To find tenants

Answer: B. To conduct inspections and verify property details

The due diligence period allows the buyer to conduct inspections and verify property details before finalizing the purchase.

➡️**19. What does the term 'equity' refer to in real estate?**

A. The market value of a property

B. The difference between the property's market value and the outstanding loan amount

C. The annual rental income

D. The initial down payment

Answer: B. The difference between the property's market value and the outstanding loan amount

Equity is the difference between the market value of the property and the amount still owed on any loans.

➡️**20. What is a 'contingency' in a real estate contract?**

A. A binding agreement

B. A penalty for late payment

C. A condition that must be met for the contract to proceed

D. An optional add-on to the contract

Answer: C. A condition that must be met for the contract to proceed

A contingency is a condition or action that must be met for a real estate contract to become binding.

→21. What is the primary advantage of a 'fixed-rate mortgage'?

    A. Lower initial payments

    B. Flexibility in payment amounts

    C. Interest rate remains constant

    D. No down payment required

Answer: C. Interest rate remains constant

The main advantage of a fixed-rate mortgage is that the interest rate remains constant over the life of the loan.

→22. What is the 'appraisal' primarily used for in real estate?

    A. To assess property taxes

    B. To determine the market value of a property

    C. To calculate the ROI

    D. To evaluate the property's condition

Answer: B. To determine the market value of a property

An appraisal is primarily used to determine the market value of a property, often for lending purposes.

→23. What does 'underwriting' refer to in the context of real estate financing?

    A. The process of verifying loan documents

    B. The process of evaluating a borrower's creditworthiness

    C. The drafting of the mortgage contract

    D. The calculation of interest rates

Answer: B. The process of evaluating a borrower's creditworthiness

Underwriting refers to the process where a lender evaluates the creditworthiness of a potential borrower.

➥24. What is 'cash flow' in the context of real estate investment?

A. The total value of the property

B. The money generated after all expenses are paid

C. The initial investment amount

D. The annual property tax

Answer: B. The money generated after all expenses are paid

Cash flow is the money left over after all expenses, including mortgage payments and maintenance, are paid.

➥25. What does 'closing costs' include in a real estate transaction?

A. Only the down payment

B. Only the broker's commission

C. Various fees like loan origination, appraisal, and legal fees

D. Only property taxes

Answer: C. Various fees like loan origination, appraisal, and legal fees

Closing costs include a variety of fees such as loan origination fees, appraisal fees, and legal fees, among others.

➥26. What is the primary purpose of a 'cap rate' in real estate investment?

A. To measure the risk associated with the property

B. To calculate the property taxes

C. To determine the mortgage interest rate

D. To assess the property's condition

Answer: A. To measure the risk associated with the property

The cap rate is used to measure the risk and potential return of a real estate investment.

27. What does 'amortization' refer to in a mortgage context?

A. The process of increasing property value

B. The process of paying off debt over time

C. The initial down payment

D. The annual property tax

Answer: B. The process of paying off debt over time

Amortization refers to the gradual reduction of a debt over a specified period.

28. What is a 'balloon mortgage'?

A. A mortgage with no down payment

B. A mortgage with a large final payment

C. A mortgage with fluctuating interest rates

D. A mortgage paid off in two years

Answer: B. A mortgage with a large final payment

A balloon mortgage requires a large lump-sum payment at the end of the loan term.

29. What does 'leverage' mean in real estate investment?

A. Using borrowed funds for investment

B. Increasing the property's value through improvements

C. The ratio of debt to equity

D. The annual rental income

Answer: A. Using borrowed funds for investment

Leverage refers to the use of borrowed funds to finance a real estate investment.

30. What is 'escrow' in a real estate transaction?

A. A legal agreement between buyer and seller

B. An account where funds are held until the transaction is completed

C. The commission paid to the real estate agent

D. The initial offer made by the buyer

Answer: B. An account where funds are held until the transaction is completed

Escrow is an account where funds are held by a third party until specific conditions are met.

➡ **31. What is the 'loan-to-value ratio' used for?**

A. To determine the interest rate

B. To calculate the down payment

C. To assess the risk of the loan

D. To measure property appreciation

Answer: C. To assess the risk of the loan

The loan-to-value ratio is used by lenders to evaluate the risk associated with a mortgage loan.

➡ **32. What does 'negative gearing' refer to in real estate investment?**

A. When rental income exceeds expenses

B. When expenses exceed rental income

C. When the property value decreases

D. When the mortgage is paid off

Answer: B. When expenses exceed rental income

Negative gearing occurs when the costs of owning a property exceed the income it generates.

➡ **33. What is a '1031 exchange'?**

A. A tax-deferred property exchange

B. A type of mortgage

C. A property valuation method

D. A type of property insurance

Answer: A. A tax-deferred property exchange

A 1031 exchange allows the owner to sell a property and reinvest the proceeds in a new property while deferring capital gains tax.

➡️**34. What is 'equity' in a property?**

A. The market value of the property

B. The amount owed on the mortgage

C. The property's purchase price

D. The difference between the property's value and the mortgage balance

Answer: D. The difference between the property's value and the mortgage balance

Equity is the value of ownership interest in the property, calculated as the property's market value minus the remaining mortgage balance.

➡️**35. What does 'due diligence' mean in a real estate context?**

A. The initial deposit made by the buyer

B. The research and analysis done before purchasing a property

C. The final inspection of the property

D. The negotiation process between buyer and seller

Answer: B. The research and analysis done before purchasing a property

Due diligence refers to the comprehensive appraisal and verification of a property before buying it.

➡️**36. What is a 'second mortgage'?**

A. A mortgage taken out on a second property

B. A mortgage that replaces the first one

C. An additional loan secured by the same property

D. A mortgage with a second lender

Answer: C. An additional loan secured by the same property

A second mortgage is a loan that is secured by the equity in your home, in addition to your primary mortgage.

➡37. What is 'imputed rent'?

A. Rent paid in advance

B. The rental value of a property you own and live in

C. Rent paid in installments

D. The tax on rental income

Answer: B. The rental value of a property you own and live in

Imputed rent is the economic theory of the rent you could be earning from leasing a property instead of living in it.

➡38. What is a 'fixed-rate mortgage'?

A. A mortgage with fluctuating interest rates

B. A mortgage with a constant interest rate

C. A mortgage with a variable down payment

D. A mortgage that can be paid off at any time

Answer: B. A mortgage with a constant interest rate

A fixed-rate mortgage has an interest rate that remains the same for the entire term of the loan.

➡39. What is 'redlining'?

A. A method of property valuation

B. Discriminatory practice in lending or insurance

C. A type of property insurance

D. A method of calculating mortgage interest

Answer: B. Discriminatory practice in lending or insurance

Redlining is an unethical practice where services are denied or priced differently in certain areas, often based on racial or ethnic composition.

➡**40. What is 'gross yield' in real estate investment?**

A. Annual rent divided by property value

B. Monthly rent multiplied by 12

C. Property value divided by annual rent

D. Annual rent minus expenses

Answer: A. Annual rent divided by property value

Gross yield is calculated by taking the annual rental income, dividing it by the property value, and then multiplying by 100 to get a percentage.

➡**41. What does 'amortization' refer to in a mortgage context?**

A. The process of increasing property value

B. The process of paying off debt over time

C. The process of calculating interest rates

D. The process of transferring property ownership

Answer: B. The process of paying off debt over time

Amortization refers to the gradual reduction of a debt over a given period.

➡**42. What is a 'balloon payment'?**

A. A small initial down payment

B. A large final payment at the end of a loan term

C. A monthly mortgage payment

D. An extra payment to reduce loan principal

Answer: B. A large final payment at the end of a loan term

A balloon payment is a large, lump-sum payment made at the end of a loan's term.

➡**43. What is 'capital gains tax'?**

A. Tax on rental income

B. Tax on the sale of a property

C. Tax on property purchase

D. Tax on mortgage interest

Answer: B. Tax on the sale of a property

Capital gains tax is levied on the profit made from selling a property.

➡**44. What is a 'contingency' in a real estate contract?**

A. A penalty clause

B. A condition that must be met for the contract to proceed

C. A fixed closing date

D. A mandatory down payment

Answer: B. A condition that must be met for the contract to proceed

A contingency is a condition or action that must be met for a real estate contract to become binding.

➡**45. What is 'escrow'?**

A. A type of mortgage

B. A legal arrangement where a third party holds assets

C. A method of property valuation

D. A type of property insurance

Answer: B. A legal arrangement where a third party holds assets

Escrow is a legal concept where a financial instrument or asset is held by a third party on behalf of two other parties in a transaction.

➡**46. What is 'net operating income' in real estate?**

A. Gross income minus expenses

B. Gross income plus expenses

C. Property value minus mortgage

D. Annual rent divided by property value

Answer: A. Gross income minus expenses

Net operating income is the total income generated by a property, minus the operating expenses.

➡**47. What does 'underwriting' refer to in real estate?**

A. The process of property valuation

B. The process of assessing the risk of a loan

C. The process of property inspection

D. The process of transferring property ownership

Answer: B. The process of assessing the risk of a loan

Underwriting is the process by which a lender evaluates the risk of offering a mortgage loan.

➡**48. What is 'zoning' in real estate?**

A. The process of property valuation

B. The division of land into areas for specific uses

C. The process of property inspection

D. The process of transferring property ownership

Answer: B. The division of land into areas for specific uses

Zoning refers to municipal or local laws or regulations that dictate how real property can and cannot be used in certain areas.

➡**49. What is 'leverage' in real estate investment?**

A. Using borrowed funds for investment

B. The ratio of debt to equity

C. The process of property valuation

D. The process of property inspection

Answer: A. Using borrowed funds for investment

Leverage in real estate refers to using borrowed capital for the purpose of expanding the potential return of an investment.

➡**50. What is a 'real estate bubble'?**

A. A period of rapid increase in property value

B. A period of rapid decrease in property value

C. A stable real estate market

D. A period of high rental income

Answer: A. A period of rapid increase in property value

A real estate bubble refers to a period of speculative excess where property prices rise rapidly and unsustainably.

Financing

Financing is a cornerstone of real estate transactions, and understanding its intricacies is crucial for anyone looking to buy or sell property in New Jersey. This chapter aims to provide a comprehensive guide on various financing options, the mortgage process, and New Jersey-specific regulations that could affect your financing decisions.

Types of Financing Options

Conventional Loans

Conventional loans are not backed by any government entity and are the most straightforward type of mortgage. They usually require a down payment of at least 20% and a good credit score.

FHA Loans

Federal Housing Administration (FHA) loans are government-backed and are ideal for first-time homebuyers or those with less-than-perfect credit. The down payment can be as low as 3.5%.

VA Loans

Veterans Affairs (VA) loans are available to veterans and active-duty military personnel. These loans require no down payment and no private mortgage insurance (PMI).

USDA Loans

These are loans backed by the United States Department of Agriculture and are designed for rural properties. They offer 100% financing and reduced mortgage insurance costs.

The Mortgage Process

Pre-Approval

Before you start house hunting, it's advisable to get pre-approved for a mortgage. This will give you an idea of how much you can afford and show sellers that you are a serious buyer.

Loan Application

Once you've found a property, the next step is to fill out a loan application. You'll need to provide various documents like W-2 forms, bank statements, and tax returns.

Underwriting

The underwriter will review your application and assess the risk of lending to you. They will look at your credit score, debt-to-income ratio, and the appraised value of the property.

Closing

This is the final step in the mortgage process. You'll sign all the necessary documents, make your down payment, and pay any closing costs. After this, the loan amount will be disbursed to the seller.

New Jersey-Specific Regulations

Interest Rates

New Jersey does not have any state-specific regulations on mortgage interest rates, but it's essential to shop around for the best rates.

Property Taxes

New Jersey has some of the highest property taxes in the nation, which can significantly affect your monthly mortgage payments.

PMI Requirements

If your down payment is less than 20%, you'll likely have to pay PMI. However, once you've built up 20% equity in your home, you can request to have the PMI removed.

Financial Assistance Programs

First-Time Homebuyer Programs

New Jersey offers several programs to assist first-time homebuyers, including down payment assistance and reduced interest rates.

Affordable Housing Programs

There are also programs aimed at making housing more affordable for low-income families.

Case Studies

Case Study 1: Financing a Condo in Hoboken

This case study explores the process of securing a conventional loan for a condo in Hoboken, considering the high property taxes and PMI.

Case Study 2: Using an FHA Loan for a Fixer-Upper in Trenton

This case study delves into how an FHA 203(k) loan can be used to finance both the purchase and renovation of a fixer-upper.

Conclusion

Financing is a complex but crucial aspect of real estate transactions in New Jersey. Whether you're a first-time homebuyer or an experienced investor, understanding your financing options and the mortgage process can save you time and money. This chapter has aimed to provide a comprehensive overview to equip you with the knowledge you need to navigate the financing landscape in New Jersey successfully.

Mock Exam Financing

➡1. What is the minimum down payment generally required for a conventional loan?

   A. 3.5%

   B. 5%

   C. 10%

   D. 20%

Answer: D. 20%

Conventional loans usually require a higher down payment, often 20%, to avoid the need for mortgage insurance.

➡2. Which type of loan is backed by the Federal Housing Administration?

   A. Conventional Loan

   B. FHA Loan

   C. VA Loan

   D. ARM

Answer: B. FHA Loan

FHA loans are backed by the Federal Housing Administration and are designed for low-to-moderate-income borrowers.

➡3. Who is eligible for a VA loan?

   A. First-time homebuyers

   B. Veterans and active-duty military personnel

   C. Low-income borrowers

   D. Investors

Answer: B. Veterans and active-duty military personnel

VA loans are a benefit specifically for veterans and active-duty military personnel.

➡4. What is the main feature of an Adjustable-Rate Mortgage (ARM)?

    A. Fixed interest rate

    B. Lower initial interest rate

    C. No down payment

    D. Easier credit requirements

Answer: B. Lower initial interest rate

ARMs often start with lower rates than fixed-rate mortgages but the rates can increase over time.

➡5. What do interest-only loans allow you to pay initially?

    A. Only the principal

    B. Only the interest

    C. Both principal and interest

    D. Down payment only

Answer: B. Only the interest

Interest-only loans allow you to pay just the interest for a specific initial period, usually 5-10 years.

➡6. What is the first step in the mortgage process?

    A. Loan Application

    B. Pre-Approval

    C. Underwriting

    D. Closing

Answer: B. Pre-Approval

Before looking at properties, it's advisable to get pre-approved for a mortgage, which involves a lender checking your financial background.

➡7. What does the underwriting process involve?

   A. Property inspection

   B. Financial due diligence

   C. Property selection

   D. Loan repayment

Answer: B. Financial due diligence

During underwriting, the lender assesses your financial situation in detail and checks the property appraisal.

➡8. What is usually included in closing costs?

   A. Monthly mortgage payments

   B. Down payment

   C. Loan origination fees

   D. Property taxes

Answer: C. Loan origination fees

Closing costs can include loan origination fees, appraisal fees, title searches, and more.

➡9. What can significantly impact your monthly mortgage payments?

   A. Type of property

   B. Real estate agent's commission

   C. Interest rates

   D. Home inspection fees

Answer: C. Interest rates

The interest rate on your mortgage will significantly impact your monthly payments and the overall cost of the loan.

➡10. What is often included in monthly mortgage payments and paid by the lender annually?

    A. Closing costs

    B. Down payment

    C. Property taxes and homeowner's insurance

    D. Mortgage insurance

Answer: C. Property taxes and homeowner's insurance

Property taxes and homeowner's insurance are often included in monthly mortgage payments and are then paid by the lender on an annual basis.

➡11. What is the purpose of a good faith estimate?

    A. To provide an estimate of closing costs

    B. To lock in an interest rate

    C. To guarantee loan approval

    D. To assess property value

    Answer: A. To provide an estimate of closing costs

    A good faith estimate is provided by the lender to give you an idea of your closing costs.

➡12. What is a balloon mortgage?

    A. A mortgage with fluctuating interest rates

    B. A mortgage that requires a large payment at the end

    C. A mortgage with no down payment

    D. A mortgage with very low monthly payments

Answer: B. A mortgage that requires a large payment at the end

A balloon mortgage requires a large lump sum payment at the end of the loan term.

➡️13. What does LTV stand for?

A. Loan To Value

B. Long Term Viability

C. Loan Transfer Variable

D. Low Transaction Volume

Answer: A. Loan To Value

LTV stands for Loan To Value, which is the ratio of the loan amount to the value of the property.

➡️14. What is a home equity loan?

A. A loan for first-time homebuyers

B. A loan based on the value of your home

C. A loan for home repairs

D. A loan for investment properties

Answer: B. A loan based on the value of your home

A home equity loan is a type of loan where the borrower uses the equity of their home as collateral.

➡️15. What is PMI?

A. Property Management Insurance

B. Private Mortgage Insurance

C. Public Mortgage Index

D. Property Maintenance Inclusion

Answer: B. Private Mortgage Insurance

PMI stands for Private Mortgage Insurance, which is usually required when the down payment is less than 20%.

➡16. What is a reverse mortgage?

A. A mortgage for seniors to convert equity into cash

B. A mortgage with reverse interest rates

C. A mortgage that pays the borrower

D. A mortgage for investment properties

Answer: A. A mortgage for seniors to convert equity into cash

A reverse mortgage allows seniors to convert the equity in their home into cash, usually for living expenses.

➡17. What is the main advantage of a 15-year mortgage over a 30-year mortgage?

A. Lower interest rates

B. Lower monthly payments

C. No down payment

D. No closing costs

Answer: A. Lower interest rates

A 15-year mortgage typically offers lower interest rates and allows you to build equity faster.

➡18. What does refinancing a mortgage mean?

A. Changing the terms of your mortgage

B. Extending your mortgage term

C. Taking out a second mortgage

D. Defaulting on your mortgage

Answer: A. Changing the terms of your mortgage

Refinancing involves replacing your existing mortgage with a new one, usually with better terms.

➡19. What is a credit score primarily used for in the mortgage process?

    A. To determine eligibility for certain types of loans

    B. To decide the size of the down payment

    C. To set the property value

    D. To calculate closing costs

Answer: A. To determine eligibility for certain types of loans

Your credit score is used to determine your eligibility for loans and the interest rate you'll receive.

➡20. What is a jumbo loan?

    A. A loan for small properties

    B. A loan exceeding conforming loan limits

    C. A loan for commercial properties

    D. A loan for mobile homes

Answer: B. A loan exceeding conforming loan limits

A jumbo loan is a mortgage that exceeds the conforming loan limits set by federal agencies.

➡21. What is the primary purpose of an escrow account in a mortgage?

    A. To hold the down payment

    B. To pay property taxes and insurance

    C. To cover repair costs

    D. To pay off the mortgage early

Answer: B. To pay property taxes and insurance

An escrow account is typically used to hold funds for paying property taxes and insurance.

→22. **What is an adjustable-rate mortgage (ARM)?**

　　A. A mortgage with a fixed interest rate

　　B. A mortgage with an interest rate that can change

　　C. A mortgage with no interest

　　D. A mortgage for investment properties

Answer: B. A mortgage with an interest rate that can change

An adjustable-rate mortgage has an interest rate that can change periodically depending on market conditions.

→23. **What is the debt-to-income ratio?**

　　A. The ratio of your monthly debt payments to your monthly income

　　B. The ratio of your loan amount to your property value

　　C. The ratio of your credit score to your income

　　D. The ratio of your down payment to your loan amount

Answer: A. The ratio of your monthly debt payments to your monthly income

The debt-to-income ratio is used by lenders to assess your ability to manage payments.

→24. **What is a pre-qualification in the mortgage process?**

　　A. A binding agreement between you and the lender

　　B. An estimate of how much you can borrow

　　C. A guarantee of a loan

　　D. A final approval for a loan

Answer: B. An estimate of how much you can borrow

Pre-qualification is an initial step that gives you an estimate of how much you may be able to borrow.

➡ **25. What is the main disadvantage of an interest-only mortgage?**

    A. You can't pay off the principal

    B. You pay more interest over time

    C. You can't refinance

    D. You need a large down payment

Answer: B. You pay more interest over time

With an interest-only mortgage, you end up paying more in interest because you're not reducing the principal.

➡ **26. What does APR stand for?**

    A. Annual Property Rate

    B. Annual Percentage Rate

    C. Approved Payment Rate

    D. Average Price Range

Answer: B. Annual Percentage Rate

APR stands for Annual Percentage Rate, which includes the interest rate and other loan costs.

➡ **27. What is a conforming loan?**

    A. A loan that meets federal guidelines

    B. A loan for investment properties

    C. A loan with no down payment

    D. A loan with a variable interest rate

Answer: A. A loan that meets federal guidelines

A conforming loan is one that adheres to the guidelines set by Fannie Mae and Freddie Mac.

➡️**28. What is a VA loan?**

    A. A loan for veterans

    B. A loan for vacation homes

    C. A loan for very large properties

    D. A loan for agricultural properties

Answer: A. A loan for veterans

A VA loan is a mortgage loan in the United States guaranteed by the United States Department of Veterans Affairs.

➡️**29. What is the main advantage of a fixed-rate mortgage?**

    A. Lower interest rates

    B. Interest rate can decrease

    C. Monthly payments stay the same

    D. No down payment required

Answer: C. Monthly payments stay the same

With a fixed-rate mortgage, your monthly payments are predictable because the interest rate stays the same.

➡️**30. What is underwriting in the context of mortgages?**

    A. The process of verifying financial information

    B. The process of selling a mortgage

    C. The process of setting interest rates

    D. The process of inspecting a property

Answer: A. The process of verifying financial information

Underwriting involves verifying your financial information and assessing the risk of offering you a loan.

➡ **31. What is a balloon payment?**

    A. A small monthly payment

    B. A large final payment

    C. A payment made annually

    D. A payment made bi-weekly

Answer: B. A large final payment

A balloon payment is a large, lump-sum payment made at the end of a loan term.

➡ **32. What is the purpose of private mortgage insurance (PMI)?**

    A. To protect the borrower from foreclosure

    B. To protect the lender if the borrower defaults

    C. To lower the interest rate

    D. To eliminate the need for a down payment

Answer: B. To protect the lender if the borrower defaults

PMI is designed to protect the lender in case the borrower defaults on the loan.

➡ **33. What is the primary purpose of an amortization schedule?**

    A. To show the breakdown of each monthly payment into principal and interest

    B. To show the total amount of interest paid over the life of the loan

    C. To show the property's appreciation value over time

    D. To show the borrower's credit score

Answer: A. To show the breakdown of each monthly payment into principal and interest

An amortization schedule provides a detailed breakdown of each monthly payment, showing how much goes toward the principal and how much goes toward interest.

➡34. What is a fixed-rate mortgage?

A. A mortgage with an interest rate that changes over time

B. A mortgage with a constant interest rate for the life of the loan

C. A mortgage with varying monthly payments

D. A mortgage with no interest

Answer: B. A mortgage with a constant interest rate for the life of the loan

A fixed-rate mortgage has an interest rate that remains the same for the entire term of the loan, providing predictability in payments.

➡35. What is a home equity line of credit (HELOC)?

A. A fixed-rate loan

B. A revolving line of credit

C. A type of insurance

D. A government grant

Answer: B. A revolving line of credit

A HELOC is a revolving line of credit that uses your home as collateral.

➡36. What is the loan-to-value ratio (LTV)?

A. The ratio of the loan amount to the property value

B. The ratio of the down payment to the loan amount

C. The ratio of the interest rate to the loan amount

D. The ratio of the loan amount to the borrower's income

Answer: A. The ratio of the loan amount to the property value

The loan-to-value ratio is the amount of the loan compared to the value of the property.

➡ **37. What is a subprime mortgage?**

    A. A mortgage for borrowers with excellent credit

    B. A mortgage for borrowers with poor credit

    C. A mortgage with no interest

    D. A mortgage for commercial properties

Answer: B. A mortgage for borrowers with poor credit

A subprime mortgage is designed for borrowers who have poor credit history.

➡ **38. What is refinancing?**

    A. Taking out a second mortgage

    B. Replacing an existing loan with a new one

    C. Changing the terms of your existing loan

    D. Selling your mortgage to another lender

Answer: B. Replacing an existing loan with a new one

Refinancing involves replacing an existing loan with a new one, usually with better terms.

➡ **39. What is a bridge loan?**

    A. A loan for construction projects

    B. A short-term loan to cover the period between two long-term loans

    C. A loan for first-time homebuyers

    D. A loan for renovating a property

Answer: B. A short-term loan to cover the period between two long-term loans

A bridge loan is a short-term loan used until a person secures permanent financing.

➡40. What is a seller carry-back?

    A. When the seller pays the closing costs

    B. When the seller acts as the lender

    C. When the seller pays for repairs

    D. When the seller pays the agent's commission

Answer: B. When the seller acts as the lender

In a seller carry-back, the seller provides financing to the buyer, essentially acting as the lender.

➡41. What is the Loan-to-Value (LTV) ratio?

    A. The ratio of the loan amount to the property's appraised value

    B. The ratio of the loan amount to the borrower's income

    C. The ratio of the property's appraised value to the market value

    D. The ratio of the down payment to the loan amount

Answer: A. The ratio of the loan amount to the property's appraised value

The Loan-to-Value (LTV) ratio is calculated by dividing the loan amount by the property's appraised value.

➡42. What does a balloon payment refer to?

    A. A large final payment at the end of a loan term

    B. Monthly payments that gradually decrease

    C. An initial down payment

    D. Monthly payments that gradually increase

Answer: A. A large final payment at the end of a loan term

A balloon payment is a large, lump-sum payment made at the end of a loan's term.

➡43. What is the purpose of a "good faith estimate" in mortgage lending?

    A. To provide an estimate of closing costs

    B. To lock in an interest rate

    C. To assess the borrower's creditworthiness

    D. To determine the property's market value

Answer: A. To provide an estimate of closing costs

A "good faith estimate" is provided by the lender to give the borrower an estimate of the closing costs involved in the mortgage process.

➡44. What does the term "amortization" refer to in the context of a mortgage?

    A. The process of increasing the loan amount

    B. The process of paying off the loan over time

    C. The process of adjusting the interest rate

    D. The process of transferring the loan to another lender

Answer: B. The process of paying off the loan over time.

Amortization refers to the process of gradually paying off a loan over a specified period, usually through regular payments that cover both principal and interest.

➡45. What is the primary advantage of a fixed-rate mortgage over an adjustable-rate mortgage?

    A. Lower initial interest rate

    B. Interest rate can decrease over time

    C. Interest rate remains constant over the loan term

    D. Easier qualification criteria

Answer: C. Interest rate remains constant over the loan term

The primary advantage of a fixed-rate mortgage is that the interest rate remains constant over the term of the loan, providing predictability in payments.

➡46. What is private mortgage insurance (PMI)?

A. Insurance that protects the lender

B. Insurance that protects the borrower

C. Insurance that protects the property

D. Insurance that protects against natural disasters

Answer: A. Insurance that protects the lender

PMI is insurance that protects the lender in case the borrower defaults on the loan.

➡47. What is an escrow account primarily used for?

A. Investing in stocks

B. Paying property taxes and insurance

C. Saving for retirement

D. Paying off the mortgage early

Answer: B. Paying property taxes and insurance

An escrow account is typically used to pay property taxes and insurance premiums.

➡48. What is a debt-to-income ratio?

A. The ratio of a borrower's total debt to total income

B. The ratio of a borrower's credit score to income

C. The ratio of a borrower's assets to liabilities

D. The ratio of a borrower's monthly expenses to income

Answer: A. The ratio of a borrower's total debt to total income

The debt-to-income ratio is calculated by dividing a borrower's total debt by their total income.

➡️49. What is the primary purpose of a rate lock?

    A. To increase the interest rate over time

    B. To decrease the interest rate over time

    C. To secure an interest rate for a specified period

    D. To allow the interest rate to fluctuate

Answer: C. To secure an interest rate for a specified period

A rate lock secures a specific interest rate for a set period, usually during the loan application process.

➡️50. What is a pre-qualification?

    A. A binding agreement between the lender and borrower

    B. An initial assessment of a borrower's creditworthiness

    C. A final approval for a loan

    D. A legal document outlining the terms of the loan

Answer: B. An initial assessment of a borrower's creditworthiness

A pre-qualification is an initial evaluation of a borrower's creditworthiness, usually based on self-reported financial information.

Transfer of Property

The transfer of property is a critical stage in any real estate transaction. It involves various legal and financial processes that both the buyer and the seller must navigate. This chapter will provide an in-depth look at the steps, documents, and laws that are specific to New Jersey when it comes to transferring property.

Types of Property Transfers

Simple Sale

This is the most common form of property transfer, where the property is sold by one party to another.

Inheritance

Property can also be transferred through inheritance, where it passes on to heirs upon the owner's death.

Gift

A property can be gifted from one individual to another, often between family members.

Foreclosure

In cases where the property owner defaults on their mortgage payments, the property may be transferred to the bank or lender through foreclosure.

Legal Documents Involved

Deed

The deed is the most crucial document in the transfer of property. In New Jersey, the most commonly used deeds are the warranty deed and the quitclaim deed.

Bill of Sale

This document outlines the terms and conditions of the property sale, including the sale price and date of transfer.

Affidavit of Title

This is a sworn statement by the seller, confirming that they are the rightful owner of the property and that there are no legal hindrances to the sale.

Steps in the Transfer Process

Contract of Sale

The first step in transferring property is the signing of a contract of sale. This contract outlines the terms agreed upon by both parties.

Due Diligence

Both parties should conduct due diligence to ensure that all legal and financial aspects of the property are in order.

Closing

The closing is the final step in the transfer process. It involves the signing of all necessary documents and the payment of the sale price and any additional fees.

New Jersey-Specific Regulations

Attorney Review

In New Jersey, both the buyer and the seller have the right to have an attorney review the contract of sale within three days of its signing.

Transfer Taxes

New Jersey imposes both a state and a county transfer tax on the sale of real estate.

Disclosure Requirements

New Jersey law requires sellers to disclose any known material defects in the property.

Common Issues and How to Avoid Them

Title Issues

One of the most common issues in property transfer is a clouded title. It's crucial to conduct a thorough title search to avoid this.

Financing Delays

Ensure that all financing is in place before the closing to avoid any last-minute delays.

Inspection Failures

Always have the property inspected before the closing to identify any issues that may need to be addressed.

Case Studies

Case Study 1: Transfer of a Multi-Family Home in Newark

This case study will delve into the complexities involved in transferring a multi-family home, including zoning laws and multiple tenants.

Case Study 2: Inheritance and Transfer of a Beachfront Property

Inheriting a property comes with its own set of challenges and responsibilities, as this case study will explore.

Conclusion

The transfer of property in New Jersey involves multiple steps and documents, each with its own set of rules and regulations. Whether you're a buyer or a seller, understanding these can help you navigate the process more smoothly and avoid common pitfalls. This chapter aims to serve as a comprehensive guide to help you understand all that's involved in the transfer of property in New Jersey.

Mock Exam Transfer of Property

➡1. **What is the most common form of voluntary property transfer?**

    A. Foreclosure

    B. Eminent Domain

    C. Sales

    D. Adverse Possession

Answer: C. Sales

Sales are the most common form of voluntary property transfer, usually involving a straightforward transaction between a buyer and a seller.

➡2. **Which type of deed offers the least protection to the buyer?**

    A. General Warranty Deed

    B. Special Warranty Deed

    C. Quitclaim Deed

    D. Bargain and Sale Deed

Answer: C. Quitclaim Deed

Quitclaim Deeds offer the least protection as they come with no warranties.

➡3. **What is the legal process by which a lender can take possession of a property due to default?**

    A. Eminent Domain

    B. Foreclosure

    C. Adverse Possession

    D. Gifting

Answer: B. Foreclosure

Foreclosure is the legal process that allows a lender to take possession of a property when the owner defaults on mortgage payments.

➡️**4. What is the minimum requirement for a deed to be enforceable?**

    A. Oral Agreement

    B. Written Instrument

    C. Mutual Consent

    D. Legal Capacity

Answer: B. Written Instrument

A deed must be in writing to be legally enforceable, complying with state laws.

➡️**5. What does a Preliminary Title Report outline?**

    A. Tax implications of the sale

    B. Issues with the title

    C. Financing options

    D. Property valuation

Answer: B. Issues with the title

A Preliminary Title Report outlines any issues with the title that need to be resolved before the sale can proceed.

➡️**6. What is the purpose of opening an escrow account?**

    A. To hold funds and documents related to the transaction

    B. To pay property taxes

    C. To hold the seller's profit

    D. To pay the real estate agent's commission

Answer: A. To hold funds and documents related to the transaction

An escrow account is opened to securely hold funds and documents related to the property transaction until all conditions are met.

➡7. What is the term for gaining ownership of a property by occupying it for an extended period under certain conditions?

    A. Eminent Domain

    B. Foreclosure

    C. Adverse Possession

    D. Inheritance

Answer: C. Adverse Possession

Adverse Possession allows someone to gain ownership of a property by occupying it for an extended period, provided certain legal conditions are met.

➡8. What type of deed only covers the period of the current owner's tenure?

    A. General Warranty Deed

    B. Special Warranty Deed

    C. Quitclaim Deed

    D. Bargain and Sale Deed

Answer: B. Special Warranty Deed

A Special Warranty Deed only covers the period of the current owner's tenure and does not extend back to the property's origins.

➡9. What is the term for the government acquiring private property for public use?

    A. Foreclosure

    B. Eminent Domain

    C. Adverse Possession

D. Gifting

Answer: B. Eminent Domain

Eminent Domain is the legal process by which the government can acquire private property for public use, provided they offer just compensation.

➡10. What is the most common form of consideration in property transfers?

A. Services

B. Money

C. Other assets

D. Promissory notes

Answer: B. Money

Money is the most common form of consideration in property transfers, although other assets or services can also serve this purpose.

➡11. What is the term for a legal claim against a property that must be paid off when the property is sold?

A. Lien

B. Mortgage

C. Easement

D. Covenant

Answer: A. Lien

A lien is a legal claim against a property that must be paid off when the property is sold.

➡12. What is the right to use someone else's land for a specific purpose called?

A. Easement

B. Lien

C. Covenant

D. Mortgage

Answer: A. Easement

An easement grants the right to use another person's land for a specific purpose.

➡**13. What is the process of dividing a large parcel of land into smaller lots?**

A. Zoning

B. Subdivision

C. Partitioning

D. Rezoning

Answer: B. Subdivision

Subdivision is the process of dividing a larger parcel of land into smaller lots.

➡**14. What is the term for a restriction on how a property may be used?**

A. Easement

B. Covenant

C. Lien

D. Mortgage

Answer: B. Covenant

A covenant is a restriction on how a property may be used, often found in property deeds or community bylaws.

➡**15. What is the primary purpose of a title search?**

A. To determine property value

B. To find any restrictions on the property

C. To discover any liens or encumbrances on the property

D. To assess the property's condition

Answer: C. To discover any liens or encumbrances on the property

The primary purpose of a title search is to discover any liens, encumbrances, or other issues that could affect the transfer of property.

➡16. What is the term for the transfer of property upon the owner's death without a will?

A. Probate

B. Intestate

C. Testamentary

D. Inheritance

Answer: B. Intestate

When a property owner dies without a will, the property is transferred according to intestate laws.

➡17. What is the term for a change in property ownership where the new owner assumes the mortgage?

A. Assumption

B. Novation

C. Subletting

D. Foreclosure

Answer: A. Assumption

Assumption is when a new owner takes over the existing mortgage of the property.

➡18. What is the term for the right of a government or its agent to expropriate private property for public use, with payment of compensation?

A. Eminent Domain

B. Foreclosure

C. Adverse Possession

D. Lien

Answer: A. Eminent Domain

Eminent Domain is the right of a government to expropriate private property for public use, with compensation.

➡**19. What is the term for a written document that transfers title of property from one person to another?**

A. Mortgage

B. Deed

C. Lien

D. Easement

Answer: B. Deed

A deed is a written document that transfers title of property from one person to another.

➡**20. What is the term for a legal process that involves the distribution of a deceased person's property?**

A. Probate

B. Intestate

C. Foreclosure

D. Eminent Domain

Answer: A. Probate

Probate is the legal process involving the distribution of a deceased person's property, especially if they died without a will.

➡21. What is the term for acquiring property through the unauthorized occupation of another's land?

A. Adverse Possession

B. Eminent Domain

C. Foreclosure

D. Probate

Answer: A. Adverse Possession

Adverse Possession is the process of acquiring property by occupying someone else's land without permission for a certain period of time.

➡22. What is the term for a legal document that confirms the sale of a property?

A. Bill of Sale

B. Deed of Trust

C. Title Certificate

D. Warranty Deed

Answer: A. Bill of Sale

A Bill of Sale is a legal document that confirms the sale and transfer of property from one party to another.

➡23. What is the term for a legal claim by a lender on the title of a property until a debt is paid off?

A. Mortgage

B. Lien

C. Easement

D. Covenant

Answer: A. Mortgage

A mortgage is a legal claim by a lender on the title of a property until the debt secured by the mortgage is paid off.

➡24. What is the term for the legal process by which a lender takes possession of a property due to non-payment?

    A. Foreclosure
    B. Eminent Domain
    C. Probate
    D. Adverse Possession

Answer: A. Foreclosure

Foreclosure is the legal process by which a lender takes possession of a property due to the borrower's failure to make required payments.

➡25. What is the term for a legal agreement that allows one party to use another's property for a specific purpose?

    A. Lease
    B. Mortgage
    C. Easement
    D. Lien

Answer: A. Lease

A lease is a legal agreement that allows one party to use another's property for a specific period and for a specific purpose.

➡26. What is the term for the official document that records the ownership of a property?

A. Title Certificate

B. Bill of Sale

C. Deed of Trust

D. Warranty Deed

Answer: A. Title Certificate

A Title Certificate is the official document that records the ownership of a property.

➡ **27. What is the term for a legal restriction on the use of land?**

A. Zoning

B. Easement

C. Mortgage

D. Lien

Answer: A. Zoning

Zoning is a legal restriction that dictates how land in a certain area can be used.

➡ **28. What is the term for the right of a property owner to use and enjoy their property without interference?**

A. Quiet Enjoyment

B. Eminent Domain

C. Probate

D. Foreclosure

Answer: A. Quiet Enjoyment

Quiet Enjoyment is the right of a property owner to use and enjoy their property without interference from others.

➡ **29. What is the term for a legal document that outlines the terms under which a loan will be repaid?**

    A. Promissory Note
    B. Bill of Sale
    C. Title Certificate
    D. Warranty Deed

    Answer: A. Promissory Note
    A Promissory Note is a legal document that outlines the terms under which a loan will be repaid.

➡ **30. What is the term for the legal process of transferring property from a deceased person to their heirs?**

    A. Inheritance
    B. Probate
    C. Foreclosure
    D. Eminent Domain

    Answer: B. Probate
    Probate is the legal process of transferring property from a deceased person to their heirs, especially if there is no will.

➡ **31. What is the term for the legal process that allows the government to take private property for public use?**

    A. Eminent Domain
    B. Foreclosure
    C. Adverse Possession
    D. Probate

Answer: A. Eminent Domain

Eminent Domain is the legal process that allows the government to take private property for public use, usually with compensation to the owner.

➡32. What is the term for a legal agreement that secures a loan with real property?

A. Deed of Trust

B. Bill of Sale

C. Lease

D. Promissory Note

Answer: A. Deed of Trust

A Deed of Trust is a legal agreement that secures a loan with real property and serves as protection for the lender.

➡33. What is the term for the legal right to use a portion of another person's property for a specific purpose, such as a driveway or pathway?

A. Easement

B. Lien

C. Covenant

D. Right of Way

Answer: A. Easement

An easement is the legal right to use a portion of another person's property for a specific purpose, such as a driveway or pathway.

➡34. What is the term for a legal document that transfers ownership of property from the seller to the buyer?

A. Warranty Deed

B. Bill of Sale

C. Title Certificate

D. Promissory Note

Answer: A. Warranty Deed

A Warranty Deed is a legal document that transfers ownership of property from the seller to the buyer.

➟**35. What is the term for the legal right to pass through someone else's land?**

A. Right of Way

B. Easement

C. Zoning

D. Lien

Answer: A. Right of Way

Right of Way is the legal right to pass through someone else's land, often established through an easement.

➟**36. What is the term for a legal document that outlines the terms of a rental agreement?**

A. Lease Agreement

B. Bill of Sale

C. Deed of Trust

D. Promissory Note

Answer: A. Lease Agreement

A Lease Agreement is a legal document that outlines the terms of a rental agreement between a landlord and tenant.

➟**37. What is the term for the legal process of verifying the validity of a will?**

A. Probate

B. Eminent Domain

C. Foreclosure

D. Adverse Possession

Answer: A. Probate

Probate is the legal process of verifying the validity of a will and distributing the deceased's assets according to the will.

➡ **38. What is the term for a legal restriction placed on a property by a previous owner?**

A. Covenant

B. Easement

C. Lien

D. Zoning

Answer: A. Covenant

A covenant is a legal restriction placed on a property by a previous owner, often outlined in the deed.

➡ **39. What is the term for the legal process of dividing a large parcel of land into smaller lots?**

A. Subdivision

B. Zoning

C. Easement

D. Lien

Answer: A. Subdivision

Subdivision is the legal process of dividing a large parcel of land into smaller lots, often for the purpose of development.

➡40. What is the term for a legal document that grants someone the right to act on behalf of another in legal matters?

A. Power of Attorney
B. Lease Agreement
C. Deed of Trust
D. Promissory Note

Answer: A. Power of Attorney

Power of Attorney is a legal document that grants someone the right to act on behalf of another in legal matters.

➡41. What is the primary purpose of a deed restriction?

A. To limit the use of the property
B. To transfer ownership
C. To secure a loan
D. To establish easements

Answer: A. To limit the use of the property

Deed restrictions are used to limit the use of the property according to the terms set by the owner or the community.

➡42. What is the difference between a general warranty deed and a quitclaim deed?

A. A general warranty deed provides no warranties
B. A quitclaim deed provides full warranties
C. A general warranty deed provides full warranties
D. Both provide the same level of warranties

Answer: C. A general warranty deed provides full warranties

A general warranty deed provides the most protection to the buyer as it includes full warranties against any encumbrances.

➡43. What is the role of a title company in a property transaction?

A. Financing the purchase

B. Ensuring the title is clear

C. Conducting home inspections

D. Setting the property's price

Answer: B. Ensuring the title is clear

The title company ensures that the title to a piece of real estate is legitimate and then issues title insurance for that property.

➡44. What is the term for a written summary of a property's ownership history?

A. Title report

B. Chain of title

C. Deed of trust

D. Abstract of title

Answer: D. Abstract of title

An abstract of title is a written summary of a property's ownership history, which is used to determine the current status of the title.

➡45. What is the purpose of a gift deed?

A. To transfer property as a gift

B. To secure a mortgage

C. To lease the property

D. To sell the property

Answer: A. To transfer property as a gift

A gift deed is used to transfer property ownership without any exchange of money.

➡ **46. What is a defeasible fee estate?**

A. An estate that can be defeated or terminated

B. An estate that lasts forever

C. An estate that is free from encumbrances

D. An estate that is leased

Answer: A. An estate that can be defeated or terminated

A defeasible fee estate is a type of estate that can be defeated or terminated upon the occurrence of a specific event.

➡ **47. What is the primary purpose of a deed?**

A. To prove ownership of personal property

B. To transfer ownership of real property

C. To outline the terms of a mortgage

D. To establish a rental agreement

Answer: B. To transfer ownership of real property

The primary purpose of a deed is to transfer ownership of real property from one party to another. It serves as a legal document that shows the change in ownership.

➡ **48. What is the primary purpose of a land contract?**

A. To lease land

B. To sell land

C. To gift land

D. To mortgage land

Answer: B. To sell land

A land contract is primarily used to sell land, where the seller provides financing to the buyer.

➡️**49. What is the term for the right of the government to take private property for public use?**

    A. Eminent domain

    B. Escheat

    C. Foreclosure

    D. Adverse possession

Answer: A. Eminent domain

Eminent domain is the right of the government to take private property for public use, with compensation to the owner.

➡️**50. What is the process of dividing a single property into smaller parcels?**

    A. Zoning

    B. Subdivision

    C. Partition

    D. Condemnation

Answer: B. Subdivision

Subdivision is the process of dividing a single property into smaller parcels, often for the purpose of development.

Practice of Real Estate and Disclosures

The practice of real estate in New Jersey is governed by a set of laws, regulations, and ethical guidelines that aim to protect both the consumer and the real estate professionals involved. One of the most critical aspects of real estate practice is the disclosure of relevant information. This chapter will provide an in-depth look at the practice of real estate and the importance of disclosures in New Jersey.

Licensing and Continuing Education

Real Estate License

In New Jersey, practicing real estate without a license is illegal. The New Jersey Real Estate Commission (NJREC) is responsible for licensing real estate agents and brokers.

Continuing Education

New Jersey requires real estate professionals to complete continuing education courses to renew their licenses. These courses often include topics like ethics, law updates, and specialized areas of practice.

Ethical Guidelines

Code of Ethics

The National Association of Realtors (NAR) provides a Code of Ethics that all Realtors are expected to follow. This code is a comprehensive guide that outlines the professional responsibilities of Realtors.

Fiduciary Duties

Real estate agents have a fiduciary duty to their clients, meaning they must act in their clients' best interests. This includes disclosing any conflicts of interest and maintaining confidentiality.

Disclosure Requirements

Seller's Disclosure

In New Jersey, sellers are required to provide a comprehensive disclosure form that outlines any known issues with the property. This includes structural problems, environmental hazards, and any legal issues like liens or zoning restrictions.

Agent's Disclosure

Agents are required to disclose any information that could affect a client's decision to buy or sell a property. This includes any personal interest they may have in the transaction.

Dual Agency Disclosure

In cases where an agent represents both the buyer and the seller, known as a dual agency, full disclosure and written consent are required from both parties.

Fair Housing Laws

Federal Laws

The Fair Housing Act prohibits discrimination based on race, color, religion, sex, or national origin in the sale, rental, or financing of housing.

New Jersey Laws

New Jersey's Law Against Discrimination (LAD) further extends these protections to include marital status, sexual orientation, and gender identity.

Technology in Real Estate Practice

MLS Systems

Multiple Listing Service (MLS) systems are widely used in New Jersey to list properties for sale and to facilitate cooperation among agents.

Virtual Tours

The use of virtual tours and other digital marketing strategies has become increasingly common, especially in the wake of the COVID-19 pandemic.

E-Signatures

New Jersey law allows for the use of electronic signatures in real estate transactions, making the process more efficient.

Case Studies

Case Study 1: Disclosure Failures

This case study examines a situation where a seller failed to disclose a major structural issue, leading to legal repercussions.

Case Study 2: Ethical Dilemmas in Dual Agency

This case study explores the ethical complexities that arise when an agent represents both the buyer and the seller.

Conclusion

The practice of real estate in New Jersey is a complex field that requires a deep understanding of both legal and ethical guidelines. Disclosures play a critical role in ensuring that all parties are well-informed and protected. Whether you're an aspiring real estate professional or a consumer looking to buy or sell property, understanding these guidelines can help you navigate the complexities of the New Jersey real estate market.

Mock Exam Practice of Real Estate and Disclosures

➡1. What is the primary focus of residential sales in real estate practice?

A. Lease agreements

B. Market trends

C. Zoning laws

D. Property management

Answer: B

Residential sales primarily focus on understanding market trends, property values, and the needs of clients.

➡2. What does a property manager NOT typically handle?

A. Rent collection

B. Maintenance and repairs

C. Property appraisals

D. Tenant relations

Answer: C

Property managers usually do not handle property appraisals; that's the job of a certified appraiser.

➡3. What is a material fact in real estate disclosures?

A. The color of the walls

B. The age of the roof

C. The seller's reason for moving

D. The brand of appliances in the home

Answer: B

Material facts include significant issues like the age of the roof, which could affect the property's value and condition.

➡️4. What is the primary role of a leasing agent?

A. Property valuation

B. Finding tenants

C. Handling legal actions

D. Managing day-to-day operations

Answer: B

Leasing agents focus on finding tenants for vacant properties.

➡️5. What must be disclosed about homes built before 1978?

A. Asbestos

B. Radon

C. Lead-based paint

D. All of the above

Answer: C

Federal law requires the disclosure of lead-based paint for homes built before 1978.

➡️6. Who is responsible for providing a Seller's Property Disclosure?

A. Buyer

B. Seller

C. Real estate agent

D. Home inspector

Answer: B

The seller is responsible for filling out the Seller's Property Disclosure form.

➡7. What is NOT a type of disclosure in real estate?

A. Seller's Property Disclosure

B. Agency Disclosures

C. Financial Disclosures

D. Buyer's Property Disclosure

Answer: D

There is no such thing as a Buyer's Property Disclosure; the seller provides all necessary disclosures.

➡8. What does a real estate appraiser provide?

A. Legal advice

B. Estimated property value

C. Lease agreements

D. Tenant screening

Answer: B

Real estate appraisers provide an estimated value of a property.

➡9. What is included in natural hazards disclosures?

A. Property age

B. Utility availability

C. Flood risk

D. Previous owners

Answer: C

Natural hazards disclosures may include information on flood risk, earthquakes, and other natural disasters.

➡10. What is the primary ethical obligation of a real estate professional?

A. Maximizing profit

B. Acting in the best interests of their clients

C. Avoiding legal repercussions

D. Networking

Answer: B

Real estate professionals are ethically bound to act in the best interests of their clients.

➡11. What is the primary purpose of a Comparative Market Analysis (CMA)?

A. To determine property taxes

B. To set a listing price

C. To assess zoning laws

D. To evaluate mortgage options

Answer: B

A Comparative Market Analysis is primarily used to set a listing price for a property based on similar properties in the area.

➡12. What does the acronym RESPA stand for?

A. Real Estate Settlement Procedures Act

B. Residential Estate Sales Professional Association

C. Real Estate Service Providers Act

D. Residential Environmental Safety Protocol Act

Answer: A

RESPA stands for Real Estate Settlement Procedures Act, which regulates closing costs and settlement procedures.

➡13. What is the role of a fiduciary in real estate?

A. To provide financing

B. To act in the best interest of the client

C. To appraise the property

D. To market the property

Answer: B

A fiduciary is obligated to act in the best interest of the client.

➡14. What is NOT a common type of real estate fraud?

A. Property flipping

B. Equity skimming

C. False advertising

D. Open listing

Answer: D

Open listing is a type of listing agreement, not a form of real estate fraud.

➡15. What is the main purpose of a title search?

A. To find the property's market value

B. To verify the legal owner of the property

C. To assess the property's condition

D. To determine the property's zoning status

Answer: B

The main purpose of a title search is to verify the legal owner of the property.

➡16. What is a latent defect?

A. A defect that is visible during a walk-through

B. A defect that is hidden and not easily discoverable

C. A defect that has been repaired

D. A defect listed in the property disclosure

Answer: B

A latent defect is a hidden defect that is not easily discoverable during a routine inspection.

➡17. What is the primary purpose of a home inspection?

A. To assess the property's market value

B. To identify any defects or issues with the property

C. To verify the property's legal status

D. To finalize the mortgage terms

Answer: B

The primary purpose of a home inspection is to identify any defects or issues with the property.

➡18. What is a short sale?

A. A quick sale process

B. Selling the property for less than the mortgage owed

C. A sale with few contingencies

D. A sale where the buyer pays in cash

Answer: B

A short sale is when the property is sold for less than the amount owed on the mortgage.

➡19. What is earnest money?

    A. The commission for the real estate agent

    B. A deposit made by the buyer

    C. The final payment at closing

    D. Money paid for a home inspection

Answer: B

Earnest money is a deposit made by the buyer to show their serious intent to purchase the property.

➡20. What does a contingency in a real estate contract allow?

    A. Immediate possession of the property

    B. The buyer to back out under specific conditions

    C. The seller to change the listing price

    D. The real estate agent to collect a higher commission

Answer: B

A contingency allows the buyer to back out of the purchase under specific conditions without losing their earnest money.

➡21. What is the primary role of the Multiple Listing Service (MLS)?

    A. To provide mortgage rates

    B. To list properties for sale

    C. To regulate real estate agents

    D. To assess property taxes

Answer: B

The primary role of the MLS is to list properties for sale, making it easier for agents to find properties for their clients.

➡22. What is a dual agency?

A. When two agents represent the buyer

B. When one agent represents both the buyer and the seller

C. When two agents represent the seller

D. When an agent represents two buyers in the same transaction

Answer: B

Dual agency occurs when one agent represents both the buyer and the seller in a real estate transaction.

➡23. What is the main purpose of a seller's disclosure?

A. To list the price of the property

B. To disclose any known defects or issues with the property

C. To describe the property's features

D. To outline the commission rates

Answer: B

The main purpose of a seller's disclosure is to disclose any known defects or issues with the property.

➡24. What does the term "underwater mortgage" mean?

A. A mortgage with a high interest rate

B. A mortgage that is higher than the property's value

C. A mortgage for a property near a body of water

D. A mortgage that has been paid off

Answer: B

An underwater mortgage is when the remaining mortgage balance is higher than the current market value of the property.

➡ **25. What is a "pocket listing"?**

A. A listing that is not yet on the market

B. A listing that is only shared with a select group of agents

C. A listing that has been sold

D. A listing that is under contract

Answer: B

A pocket listing is a listing that is not publicly advertised and is only shared with a select group of agents.

➡ **26. What is the main purpose of a buyer's agent?**

A. To list properties for sale

B. To represent the buyer's interests

C. To conduct home inspections

D. To provide financing options

Answer: B

The main purpose of a buyer's agent is to represent the interests of the buyer in a real estate transaction.

➡ **27. What is a "balloon payment"?**

A. A small monthly payment

B. A large final payment at the end of a mortgage term

C. A payment made halfway through the mortgage term

D. A payment made to the real estate agent

Answer: B

A balloon payment is a large final payment due at the end of a mortgage term.

28. What is "redlining"?

A. Drawing property boundaries

B. Discriminatory practice in lending or insurance

C. Highlighting important clauses in a contract

D. Marking properties that are under contract

Answer: B

Redlining is a discriminatory practice where services like lending or insurance are denied or priced higher for residents of certain areas.

29. What is the main purpose of an escrow account?

A. To hold the earnest money deposit

B. To pay the real estate agent's commission

C. To store the property's title

D. To hold funds for property taxes and insurance

Answer: D

The main purpose of an escrow account is to hold funds for property taxes and insurance.

30. What is a "contingent offer"?

A. An offer that is higher than the listing price

B. An offer that is dependent on certain conditions being met

C. An offer that has been accepted but not yet closed

D. An offer that is non-negotiable

Answer: B

A contingent offer is an offer that is dependent on certain conditions being met, such as financing or a satisfactory home inspection.

➡31. What is the primary role of a "listing agent"?

A. To represent the buyer in a transaction

B. To represent the seller in a transaction

C. To conduct the home inspection

D. To provide financing options

Answer: B

The primary role of a listing agent is to represent the seller in a real estate transaction, helping them to sell their property.

➡32. What is a "short sale"?

A. A quick sale of a property

B. Selling a property for less than the mortgage owed

C. Selling a property without an agent

D. A discounted sale for a quick closing

Answer: B

A short sale is when a property is sold for less than the amount owed on the mortgage.

➡33. What is "title insurance"?

A. Insurance for property damage

B. Insurance that protects against defects in the title

C. Insurance for the mortgage lender

D. Insurance for the real estate agent

Answer: B

Title insurance protects against defects in the title to the property.

➡34. What is "earnest money"?

A. Money paid to the real estate agent

B. Money paid to secure a contract

C. Money paid for a home inspection

D. Money paid for closing costs

Answer: B

Earnest money is a deposit made to a seller to show the buyer's good faith in a transaction.

➡35. What is a "FSBO" listing?

A. For Sale By Owner

B. For Sale By Operator

C. For Sale Before Offer

D. For Sale By Order

Answer: A

FSBO stands for "For Sale By Owner," indicating that the property is being sold without a real estate agent.

➡36. What is "amortization"?

A. The process of increasing property value

B. The process of paying off a loan over time

C. The process of transferring property

D. The process of evaluating a property's worth

Answer: B

Amortization is the process of paying off a loan over time through regular payments.

➡37. What is a "home warranty"?

A. A guarantee on the home's structure

B. A guarantee on the home's appliances and systems

C. A guarantee on the home's value

D. A guarantee on the home's location

Answer: B

A home warranty is a service contract that covers the repair or replacement of important home system components and appliances.

➡**38. What is "zoning"?**

A. The process of measuring a property

B. The division of land into areas for specific uses

C. The process of evaluating a property's value

D. The process of transferring property

Answer: B

Zoning is the division of land into areas designated for specific uses, such as residential, commercial, or industrial.

➡**39. What is a "pre-approval letter"?**

A. A letter confirming the property's value

B. A letter confirming mortgage eligibility

C. A letter confirming the property's condition

D. A letter confirming the real estate agent's credentials

Answer: B

A pre-approval letter is a letter from a lender indicating that a buyer is eligible for a mortgage up to a certain amount.

➡**40. What is "escrow"?**

A. A type of mortgage

B. A legal arrangement where a third party holds assets

C. A type of home inspection

D. A type of real estate contract

Answer: B

Escrow is a legal arrangement in which a third party holds assets on behalf of the buyer and seller.

➡41. What is the purpose of a "Seller's Disclosure Statement"?

A. To disclose the seller's financial status

B. To disclose any known defects or issues with the property

C. To disclose the commission rate of the real estate agents

D. To disclose the buyer's financing options

Answer: B

The Seller's Disclosure Statement is used to disclose any known defects or issues with the property to potential buyers.

➡42. What does "dual agency" mean in real estate?

A. Two agents working for the same brokerage

B. An agent representing both the buyer and the seller

C. Two buyers competing for the same property

D. Two lenders involved in the financing

Answer: B

Dual agency occurs when a real estate agent represents both the buyer and the seller in the same transaction.

➡43. What is the primary purpose of a "title search"?

    A. To find the property's market value

    B. To check for any liens or encumbrances on the property

    C. To assess the property's condition

    D. To determine the zoning laws affecting the property

Answer: B

The primary purpose of a title search is to check for any liens or encumbrances on the property.

➡44. What does "FSBO" stand for?

    A. For Sale By Owner

    B. Full Service Brokerage Option

    C. Fixed Selling Bonus Offer

    D. Final Sale Before Offer

Answer: A

FSBO stands for "For Sale By Owner," indicating that the property is being sold directly by the owner without the representation of a real estate agent.

➡45. What is a "contingency" in a real estate contract?

    A. A mandatory clause

    B. A binding agreement

    C. A condition that must be met for the contract to proceed

    D. A non-negotiable term

Answer: C

A contingency is a condition that must be met for the contract to proceed.

➡46. What is the role of an "escrow agent"?

A. To market the property

B. To hold and disburse funds during a transaction

C. To negotiate the contract terms

D. To inspect the property

Answer: B

The role of an escrow agent is to hold and disburse funds during a real estate transaction.

➡47. What does "amortization" refer to?

A. The process of increasing property value

B. The process of paying off a loan over time

C. The process of transferring property ownership

D. The process of evaluating a property's worth

Answer: B

Amortization refers to the process of paying off a loan over time through regular payments.

➡48. What is the "right of first refusal" in a real estate context?

A. The right to refuse a home inspection

B. The right to be the first to make an offer on a property

C. The right to refuse to pay closing costs

D. The right to refuse to honor a contract

Answer: B

The right of first refusal gives a person the opportunity to be the first to make an offer on a property before the owner sells it to someone else.

➡**49. What does "encumbrance" refer to in real estate?**

A. A type of insurance policy

B. A claim or lien on a property

C. A type of mortgage loan

D. A legal restriction on property use

Answer: B

An encumbrance is a claim or lien on a property that affects its use or transfer.

➡**50. What does "under contract" mean in real estate?**

A. The property is being appraised

B. The property is available for sale

C. The property has an accepted offer but has not yet closed

D. The property is off the market

Answer: C

"Under contract" means that the property has an accepted offer but the sale has not yet closed.

Contracts

Contracts are the backbone of any real estate transaction. They provide the legal framework that dictates the obligations, rights, and expectations of each party involved. In New Jersey, as in other states, understanding the intricacies of real estate contracts is crucial for both professionals and consumers. This chapter aims to provide a comprehensive overview of contracts in the New Jersey real estate market.

Types of Real Estate Contracts

Purchase Agreements

This is the most common type of contract in real estate. It outlines the terms and conditions under which a property will be sold, including the price, closing date, and any contingencies.

Lease Agreements

These contracts are used for rental properties. They specify the terms under which a property will be rented, including rent amount, duration, and tenant responsibilities.

Option Contracts

These give a potential buyer the option to purchase a property within a specified time frame but do not obligate them to do so.

Land Contracts

Also known as "contract for deed," this is an agreement where the buyer makes payments directly to the seller until the full purchase price is paid.

Essential Elements of a Contract

Offer and Acceptance

For a contract to be valid, there must be a clear offer by one party and an unequivocal acceptance by the other.

Consideration

This refers to something of value exchanged between the parties, usually the property and the purchase price.

Legal Purpose

The contract must be for a legal purpose. For example, a contract to sell a property with illegal modifications would be invalid.

Competent Parties

Both parties must be of legal age and mentally competent to enter into a contract.

Mutual Assent

Both parties must understand and agree to the terms of the contract.

Common Clauses in New Jersey Contracts

Contingency Clauses

These are conditions that must be met for the contract to proceed, such as mortgage approval or a satisfactory home inspection.

Disclosure Clauses

New Jersey law requires sellers to disclose known defects in the property. Failure to do so can result in the contract being voided.

Escrow Clauses

These dictate the terms under which earnest money will be held and disbursed.

Inspection Clauses

These allow the buyer a specified period to conduct various inspections of the property.

Legal Requirements and Regulations

Attorney Review

New Jersey is one of the few states that require an attorney review of real estate contracts within three days of both parties signing.

Consumer Fraud Act

This act protects consumers from fraudulent practices and can apply to real estate transactions.

Statute of Frauds

In New Jersey, real estate contracts must be in writing to be enforceable.

Contract Breaches and Remedies

Types of Breaches

A breach occurs when one party fails to fulfill their obligations under the contract. This can be a minor breach, which can be easily remedied, or a material breach, which significantly affects the contract's outcome.

Legal Remedies

The injured party may seek specific performance, meaning the breaching party is compelled to fulfill their obligations, or they may seek monetary damages.

Mediation and Arbitration

Many contracts include clauses requiring mediation or arbitration in the event of a dispute, as these methods are generally faster and less expensive than litigation.

Case Studies

Case Study 1: Breach of Contract

This case study examines a situation where a buyer backed out of a contract without a valid reason, resulting in legal action.

Case Study 2: Failure to Disclose

This case study explores a situation where a seller failed to disclose a significant defect, leading to the contract being voided.

Conclusion

Understanding contracts is essential for anyone involved in the New Jersey real estate market. They provide the legal framework that protects both buyers and sellers and ensure that transactions proceed smoothly. Whether you're a seasoned professional or a first-time homebuyer, a solid grasp of contract law will serve you well in any real estate transaction.

Mock Exam Contracts

➡1. What is the primary purpose of a Purchase Agreement in real estate?

A. To outline the commission for the real estate agent

B. To set the stage for the relationship between buyer and seller

C. To provide a warranty for the property

D. To list the property on MLS

Answer: B

The Purchase Agreement serves as the cornerstone of any real estate transaction, outlining the terms and conditions between the buyer and seller.

➡2. Which type of lease requires the tenant to pay a flat rent while the landlord pays for all property charges?

A. Gross Lease

B. Net Lease

C. Triple Net Lease

D. Modified Gross Lease

Answer: A

In a Gross Lease, the tenant pays a flat rent and the landlord is responsible for all property charges.

➡3. What is "Consideration" in a contract?

A. A thoughtful gesture

B. Money or something of value exchanged

C. A legal requirement

D. A counteroffer

Answer: B

Consideration refers to something of value that is exchanged between parties in a contract. It can be money, services, or even a promise.

➡️4. What happens in a Material Breach of contract?

A. A minor failure in performance

B. A significant failure in performance

C. A legal dispute

D. Contract is automatically renewed

Answer: B

A Material Breach is a significant failure in performance that allows the other party to seek remedies.

➡️5. Which clause in a contract specifies what will happen if issues are found during an inspection?

A. Contingency Clause

B. Disclosure Clause

C. Inspection Clause

D. Arbitration Clause

Answer: C

The Inspection Clause outlines the type of inspection, who will conduct it, and what actions will be taken if issues are found.

➡️6. What does a "Straight Option" in an Option Agreement provide?

A. The right to lease the property

B. The exclusive right to purchase within a certain time

C. The right to sublease the property

D. The right to first refusal

Answer: B

A Straight Option gives the buyer the exclusive right to purchase the property within a specified time frame.

➡ **7. Who cannot legally enter into a contract?**

A. A licensed real estate agent

B. A minor

C. A property manager

D. A real estate investor

Answer: B

Minors are not legally competent to enter into contracts.

➡ **8. What is the primary purpose of Disclosure Clauses?**

A. To outline the commission structure

B. To state federal and state requirements for property disclosure

C. To specify the type of inspection

D. To set the rent amount in a lease

Answer: B

Disclosure Clauses are used to state federal and state requirements for property disclosure, such as the presence of lead paint.

➡ **9. What is a Conditional Sale Agreement?**

A. The property is sold as-is

B. The sale is conditional upon certain criteria

C. The buyer has the option to purchase later

D. The seller can back out at any time

Answer: B

A Conditional Sale Agreement means the sale is conditional upon certain criteria being met, such as the sale of the buyer's current home.

➡10. What is the legal status of a contract for illegal activities?

A. Valid

B. Null and void

C. Conditional

D. Binding

Answer: B

Contracts for illegal activities are considered null and void.

➡11. What is the role of an "Escrow Agent" in a real estate contract?

A. To market the property

B. To hold and disburse funds

C. To conduct inspections

D. To negotiate terms

Answer: B

The Escrow Agent holds and disburses funds according to the terms of the contract.

➡12. Which of the following is NOT a required element for a contract to be valid?

A. Offer and acceptance

B. Consideration

C. Legal purpose

D. Notarization

Answer: D

Notarization is not a required element for a contract to be valid.

➝13. What is the "Statute of Frauds" in relation to contracts?

A. A law that makes oral contracts illegal

B. A law that requires certain contracts to be in writing

C. A law that prevents fraudulent activities

D. A law that nullifies all previous contracts

Answer: B

The Statute of Frauds requires certain contracts, like those for real estate, to be in writing to be enforceable.

➝14. What does "Time is of the Essence" mean in a contract?

A. The contract has no expiration date

B. The contract must be executed within a specific timeframe

C. The contract can be modified at any time

D. The contract is not urgent

Answer: B

"Time is of the Essence" means that the contract must be executed within a specific timeframe, and delays could lead to penalties or termination of the contract.

➝15. What is a "Right of First Refusal"?

A. The right to reject any offer

B. The right to match or better any offer received by the seller

C. The right to be the first to view a property

D. The right to terminate a contract without penalty

Answer: B

The **Right of First Refusal** allows the holder to match or better any offer received by the seller before the property is sold to another party.

➡16. What is a "Contingent Contract"?

A. A contract that is dependent on certain conditions being met

B. A contract that is legally binding

C. A contract that has been terminated

D. A contract that is in the negotiation phase

Answer: A

A **Contingent Contract** is dependent on certain conditions being met, such as financing approval or a satisfactory home inspection.

➡17. What is "Specific Performance"?

A. A clause that specifies the responsibilities of each party

B. A legal remedy for breach of contract

C. A type of contract used in commercial real estate

D. A measure of a real estate agent's effectiveness

Answer: B

Specific Performance is a legal remedy that forces the breaching party to fulfill the terms of the contract.

➡18. What is the purpose of a "Hold Harmless Clause"?

A. To protect the buyer from market fluctuations

B. To protect one or both parties from liability for the actions of the other

C. To hold the property off the market for a specific period

D. To hold the buyer's deposit in escrow

Answer: B

A Hold Harmless Clause protects one or both parties from liability for the actions or negligence of the other party.

➡19. What is a "Bilateral Contract"?

A. A contract where only one party is obligated to perform

B. A contract where both parties are obligated to perform

C. A contract that is null and void

D. A contract that has been terminated

Answer: B

In a Bilateral Contract, both parties are obligated to perform their respective duties.

➡20. What is the "Implied Covenant of Good Faith and Fair Dealing"?

A. A written clause in every contract

B. An unwritten obligation for parties to act honestly and not cheat each other

C. A legal doctrine that makes all contracts public

D. A requirement for all contracts to be reviewed by a lawyer

Answer: B

The Implied Covenant of Good Faith and Fair Dealing is an unwritten obligation that requires parties to act honestly and not cheat or mislead each other.

➡21. What is a "Unilateral Contract"?

A. A contract where only one party is obligated to perform

B. A contract where both parties are obligated to perform

C. A contract that is null and void

D. A contract that has been terminated

Answer: A

In a Unilateral Contract, only one party is obligated to perform, while the other has the option but not the obligation to perform.

→22. What is "Liquidated Damages"?

A. The actual damages suffered due to a breach

B. A pre-determined amount to be paid in case of a breach

C. The refundable part of a deposit

D. The non-refundable part of a deposit

Answer: B

Liquidated Damages are a pre-determined amount agreed upon by the parties to be paid in case of a breach of contract.

→23. What is "Novation"?

A. The act of renewing a contract

B. The act of replacing one party in a contract with another

C. The act of nullifying a contract

D. The act of negotiating the terms of a contract

Answer: B

Novation is the act of replacing one party in a contract with another, effectively transferring the obligations to the new party.

→24. What is an "Addendum"?

A. A change to the original contract

B. A separate agreement that is included with the original contract

C. A summary of the contract

D. A legal interpretation of the contract

Answer: B

An Addendum is a separate agreement that is included with the original contract to add or clarify terms.

➡25. What is "Recission"?

A. The act of renewing a contract

B. The act of terminating a contract and restoring parties to their original positions

C. The act of transferring a contract

D. The act of amending a contract

Answer: B

Recission is the act of terminating a contract and restoring the parties to their original positions, as if the contract had never existed.

➡26. What is "Parol Evidence"?

A. Written evidence

B. Oral evidence

C. Photographic evidence

D. Video evidence

Answer: B

Parol Evidence refers to oral statements or agreements that are not included in the written contract.

➡27. What is a "Counteroffer"?

A. An acceptance of the original offer

B. A rejection of the original offer

C. A new offer made in response to an original offer

D. A legal requirement for all contracts

Answer: C

A Counteroffer is a new offer made in response to an original offer, effectively rejecting the original offer.

➡**28. What is "Earnest Money"?**

A. Money paid to confirm a contract

B. Money paid to a real estate agent

C. Money held in escrow

D. Money paid for a home inspection

Answer: A

Earnest Money is money paid to confirm a contract, showing the buyer's serious intent to purchase.

➡**29. What is "Force Majeure"?**

A. A clause that frees both parties from liability in case of an extraordinary event

B. A clause that holds both parties liable regardless of circumstances

C. A clause that allows for price negotiation

D. A clause that requires a third-party mediator

Answer: A

Force Majeure is a clause that frees both parties from liability in case of an extraordinary event, like a natural disaster, that prevents one or both parties from fulfilling the contract.

➡**30. What is "Severability"?**

A. The ability to separate a contract into individual clauses

B. The ability to terminate a contract without penalty

C. The ability to transfer a contract to another party

D. The ability to amend a contract after signing

Answer: A

Severability is the ability to separate a contract into individual clauses, so that if one clause is found to be unenforceable, the rest of the contract remains in effect.

➡31. What does "Statute of Frauds" require for a real estate contract to be enforceable?

A. Verbal agreement

B. Written and signed agreement

C. Notarized agreement

D. Witnessed agreement

Answer: B

The Statute of Frauds requires that a real estate contract must be in writing and signed by the parties to be enforceable.

➡32. What is "Specific Performance"?

A. Monetary compensation for breach of contract

B. Forcing a party to carry out the terms of the contract

C. Nullifying the contract

D. Amending the contract

Answer: B

Specific Performance is a legal remedy that forces a party to carry out the terms of the contract as agreed.

➡33. What is "Time is of the Essence" in a contract?

A. A clause that allows for flexible deadlines

B. A clause that makes deadlines strictly binding

C. A clause that nullifies the contract after a certain time

D. A clause that allows for automatic renewal of the contract

Answer: B

"Time is of the Essence" is a clause that makes deadlines strictly binding, and failure to meet them could lead to breach of contract.

➡ **34. What is an "Open Listing"?**

A. A listing agreement with multiple brokers

B. A listing agreement with one broker

C. A listing that is not publicly advertised

D. A listing that is only advertised within a brokerage

Answer: A

An Open Listing is a listing agreement where the seller can employ multiple brokers who can bring buyers to the property.

➡ **35. What is a "Net Listing"?**

A. A listing where the broker's commission is a percentage of the sale price

B. A listing where the broker keeps all amounts above a certain price

C. A listing where the broker charges a flat fee

D. A listing where the broker's commission is paid by the buyer

Answer: B

In a Net Listing, the broker agrees to sell the owner's property for a set price, and anything above that price is kept as the broker's commission.

➡ **36. What is a "Contingency" in a contract?**

A. A fixed term

B. A condition that must be met for the contract to be binding

C. A penalty for breach of contract

D. An optional term

Answer: B

A Contingency is a condition that must be met for the contract to proceed to closing.

➡37. What is "Due Diligence" in the context of a real estate contract?

A. The buyer's investigation of the property

B. The seller's disclosure of property defects

C. The broker's marketing efforts

D. The lender's appraisal of the property

Answer: A

Due Diligence refers to the buyer's investigation of the property to discover any issues that were not disclosed.

➡38. What is "Escrow"?

A. A legal process to resolve disputes

B. A third-party account where funds are held until conditions are met

C. A type of mortgage

D. A tax levied on property sales

Answer: B

Escrow is a third-party account where funds or assets are held until contractual conditions are met.

➡39. What is "Right of First Refusal"?

A. The right to be the first to purchase a property

B. The right to refuse any offer on a property

C. The right to terminate a contract

D. The right to amend a contract

Answer: A

Right of First Refusal gives a person the opportunity to be the first to purchase a property before the owner sells it to someone else.

➡️40. What is "Joint Tenancy"?

A. Ownership by one individual

B. Ownership by two or more individuals with equal shares

C. Ownership by a corporation

D. Ownership by tenants

Answer: B

Joint Tenancy is a form of ownership where two or more individuals own property with equal shares and have the right of survivorship.

➡️41. What is the primary purpose of a "Letter of Intent" in a real estate transaction?

A. To serve as a binding contract

B. To outline the terms under which a contract will be negotiated

C. To legally transfer property

D. To terminate an existing contract

Answer: B

A Letter of Intent serves to outline the terms under which the parties will negotiate a contract. It is generally not binding.

➡42. What does "Time is of the Essence" mean in a real estate contract?

A. The contract has an indefinite period

B. The contract must be executed within a specific timeframe

C. The contract can be terminated at any time

D. The contract is not time-sensitive

Answer: B

"Time is of the Essence" means that the contract must be executed within a specific timeframe, and failure to do so could result in penalties or termination of the contract.

➡43. What is the purpose of an "Addendum" in a real estate contract?

A. To correct a typo or error

B. To add additional terms or conditions

C. To terminate the contract

D. To renew the contract

Answer: B

An Addendum is used to add additional terms or conditions to an existing contract, effectively modifying it.

➡44. What is the effect of a "Waiver" in a contract?

A. It adds a new term to the contract

B. It removes a party's right to enforce a term of the contract

C. It extends the contract's duration

D. It makes the contract voidable

Answer: B

A waiver removes a party's right to enforce a particular term of the contract, essentially giving up that right.

➡45. What is "Specific Performance" in the context of a real estate contract?

A. Monetary compensation

B. Carrying out the exact terms of the contract

C. Termination of the contract

D. An optional performance

Answer: B

Specific Performance refers to carrying out the exact terms of the contract, usually enforced through a court order.

➡46. What does "Novation" mean in a contract?

A. Renewal of the contract

B. Replacement of one party with another

C. Addition of a new term

D. Termination of the contract

Answer: B

Novation means the replacement of one party in the contract with another, effectively transferring the obligations to the new party.

➡47. What does "Force Majeure" refer to in a contract?

A. A type of fraud

B. An act of God or unforeseen circumstances

C. A breach of contract

D. A type of contingency

Answer: B

Force Majeure refers to unforeseen circumstances or "acts of God" that prevent one or both parties from fulfilling the contract. It usually allows for the contract to be terminated or suspended.

➡ **48. What is the role of an "Escrow Agent"?**

A. To negotiate the contract

B. To hold and disburse funds or documents

C. To enforce the contract

D. To terminate the contract

Answer: B

An Escrow Agent holds and disburses funds or documents as per the terms of the contract.

➡ **49. What is "Right of First Refusal" in a real estate contract?**

A. The right to back out of the contract first

B. The right to match any offer received by the seller

C. The right to inspect the property first

D. The right to make the first offer on a property

Answer: B

Right of First Refusal gives a party the right to match any offer received by the seller, usually before the property is sold to another buyer.

➡ **50. What is "Earnest Money" in the context of a real estate contract?**

A. The commission for the real estate agent

B. A deposit made by the buyer to show good faith

C. The final payment made at closing

D. A refundable deposit

Answer: B

Earnest Money is a deposit made by the buyer to show good faith and secure the contract.

It is usually non-refundable and is applied to the purchase price.

Real Estate Calculations

Real estate calculations are an integral part of the real estate industry. Whether you're an agent, a buyer, or an investor, understanding the numbers is crucial. This chapter will delve into the most important calculations you'll encounter, from mortgage payments to investment returns.

Property Valuation

Comparative Market Analysis (CMA)

A Comparative Market Analysis (CMA) is the cornerstone of property valuation. It involves comparing the property in question to similar properties ("comparables" or "comps") that have recently sold in the area.

Formula:

Property Value = Average Price of Comparable Properties x (1 + Adjustment Factor)}

Why It Matters:

Understanding how to accurately perform a CMA can mean the difference between overpricing a property, causing it to sit on the market, or underpricing it and losing money.

Capitalization Rate

The capitalization rate, or cap rate, is another essential metric for property valuation, particularly for income-generating properties.

Formula:

$$\text{Cap Rate} = \frac{Net\ Operating\ Income}{Current\ Market\ Value}$$

Why It Matters:

The cap rate gives you a quick way to compare the profitability of different investment properties.

Financing Calculations

Mortgage Payments

Mortgage calculations are essential for both buyers and real estate professionals to understand.

Formula:

$$M = P \times \frac{r(1+r)^n}{(1+r)^n - 1}$$

Where :

M is the monthly payment,

P is the principal loan amount,

r is the monthly interest rate, and

n is the number of payments.

Why It Matters:

Knowing how to calculate mortgage payments allows you to assess the affordability of a property and helps in planning long-term finances.

Loan-to-Value Ratio (LTV)

The Loan-to-Value ratio is a risk assessment metric that lenders use.

Formula:

$$LTV = \frac{Loan\ Amount}{Appraised\ Value} \times 100$$

Why It Matters:

A high LTV ratio might mean a riskier loan from a lender's perspective, potentially requiring the borrower to purchase mortgage insurance.

Investment Calculations

- Return on Investment (ROI)

ROI is a measure of the profitability of an investment.

Formula:

$$\text{ROI} = \frac{Net\ Profit}{Cost\ of\ Investment} \times 100$$

Why It Matters:

ROI gives you a snapshot of the investment's performance, helping you compare it against other investment opportunities.

Cash-on-Cash Return

This metric gives you the annual return on your investment based on the cash flow and the amount of money you've invested.

Formula:

$$\text{Cash-on-Cash Return} = \frac{Annual\ Cash\ Flow}{Total\ Cash\ Invested} \times 100$$

Why It Matters:

Cash-on-cash return is crucial for understanding the cash income you're generating compared to the cash invested, providing a more accurate picture of an investment's performance.

Area and Volume Calculations

Square Footage

Square footage is the measure of an area, and it's one of the most basic calculations in real estate.

Formula:

Area = Length x Width

Why It Matters:
Square footage affects everything from listing prices to renovation costs, so getting it right is crucial.

Cubic Footage

Cubic footage is often used in commercial real estate to determine the volume of a space.

Formula:

Volume = Length x Width x Height

Why It Matters:
In commercial settings, cubic footage can be essential for understanding how a space can be used.

Prorations and Commissions

Prorations
Prorations are used to divide property taxes, insurance premiums, or other costs between the buyer and seller.

Formula:

Proration Amount = $\dfrac{Annual\ Cost}{365}$ **x Number of Days**

Why It Matters:

Prorations ensure that both parties are only paying for their share of the costs during the time they own the property.

Commission Calculation

Commissions are the lifeblood of most real estate agents and brokers.

Formula:

Commission = Sale Price x Commission Rate

Why It Matters:

Understanding how commissions are calculated can help agents set realistic business goals and expectations.

Conclusion

Mastering these calculations is not just a requirement for passing various real estate exams; it's a necessity for a successful career in real estate. This chapter has covered the essential calculations any real estate professional needs to understand.

Mock Exam Real Estate Calculations

➡1. What is the formula for calculating the Loan-to-Value ratio?

   A. Loan Amount / Appraised Value

   B. Appraised Value / Loan Amount

   C. Loan Amount × Appraised Value

   D. Appraised Value × Loan Amount

Answer: A

The Loan-to-Value ratio is calculated as Loan Amount divided by Appraised Value.

➡2. What does ROI stand for?

   A. Return On Investment

   B. Rate Of Interest

   C. Real Estate Opportunity

   D. Rate Of Inflation

Answer: A

ROI stands for Return On Investment, which measures the profitability of an investment.

➡3. What is the formula for calculating square footage?

   A. Length × Width

   B. Length × Height

   C. Length + Width

   D. Length / Width

Answer: A

Square footage is calculated by multiplying the length by the width of the area.

➡4. What is the formula for calculating mortgage payments?

    A. $P \times (r(1+r)^n) / ((1+r)^n-1)$

    B. $P \times r \times n$

    C. $P / r \times n$

    D. $P \times n / r$

Answer: A

The formula for calculating mortgage payments is $P \times (r(1+r)^n) / ((1+r)^n-1)$.

➡5. What is the formula for calculating the capitalization rate?

    A. Net Operating Income / Current Market Value

    B. Current Market Value / Net Operating Income

    C. Net Operating Income $\times$ Current Market Value

    D. Current Market Value $\times$ Net Operating Income

Answer: A

The capitalization rate is calculated as Net Operating Income divided by Current Market Value.

➡6. What does CMA stand for in real estate calculations?

    A. Comparative Market Analysis

    B. Capital Market Assessment

    C. Current Market Appraisal

    D. Comparative Monetary Assessment

Answer: A

CMA stands for Comparative Market Analysis, used for property valuation.

➡7. What is the formula for calculating Cash-on-Cash Return?

A. Annual Cash Flow / Total Cash Invested × 100

B. Total Cash Invested / Annual Cash Flow × 100

C. Annual Cash Flow × Total Cash Invested

D. Total Cash Invested × Annual Cash Flow

Answer: A

Cash-on-Cash Return is calculated as Annual Cash Flow divided by Total Cash Invested, multiplied by 100.

➡8. What is the formula for calculating prorations?

A. Annual Cost / 365 × Number of Days

B. Annual Cost × 365 / Number of Days

C. Number of Days / Annual Cost × 365

D. Number of Days × Annual Cost / 365

Answer: A

Prorations are calculated as Annual Cost divided by 365, multiplied by the Number of Days.

➡9. What is the formula for calculating cubic footage?

A. Length × Width × Height

B. Length × Width

C. Length × Height

D. Width × Height

Answer: A

Cubic footage is calculated by multiplying the length, width, and height of the space.

➡10. What is the formula for calculating commissions?

A. Sale Price × Commission Rate

B. Commission Rate × Sale Price

C. Sale Price / Commission Rate

D. Commission Rate / Sale Price

Answer: A

Commissions are calculated as Sale Price multiplied by Commission Rate.

➡11. What is the formula for calculating Gross Rent Multiplier (GRM)?

A. Property Price / Gross Annual Rents

B. Gross Annual Rents / Property Price

C. Property Price × Gross Annual Rents

D. Gross Annual Rents × Property Price

Answer: A

The Gross Rent Multiplier (GRM) is calculated by dividing the property price by the gross annual rents.

➡12. What is the formula for calculating depreciation?

A. (Cost of the Property - Salvage Value) / Useful Life

B. (Salvage Value - Cost of the Property) / Useful Life

C. Cost of the Property × Salvage Value

D. Salvage Value × Cost of the Property

Answer: A

Depreciation is calculated by subtracting the salvage value from the cost of the property and dividing by its useful life.

➡13. What does PITI stand for in mortgage calculations?

A. Principal, Interest, Taxes, Insurance

B. Payment, Interest, Taxes, Insurance

C. Principal, Income, Taxes, Insurance

D. Payment, Income, Taxes, Insurance

Answer: A

PITI stands for Principal, Interest, Taxes, and Insurance, which are the four components of a mortgage payment.

➡14. What is the formula for calculating equity?

A. Market Value - Mortgage Balance

B. Mortgage Balance - Market Value

C. Market Value × Mortgage Balance

D. Mortgage Balance × Market Value

Answer: A

Equity is calculated as the market value of the property minus the mortgage balance.

➡15. What is the formula for calculating net operating income (NOI)?

A. Gross Income - Operating Expenses

B. Operating Expenses - Gross Income

C. Gross Income × Operating Expenses

D. Operating Expenses × Gross Income

Answer: A

Net Operating Income (NOI) is calculated by subtracting operating expenses from gross income.

➡16. What is the formula for calculating the break-even point?

A. Fixed Costs / (Selling Price - Variable Costs)

B. (Selling Price - Variable Costs) / Fixed Costs

C. Fixed Costs × (Selling Price - Variable Costs)

D. (Selling Price - Variable Costs) × Fixed Costs

Answer: A

The break-even point is calculated by dividing fixed costs by the difference between the selling price and variable costs.

➡17. What is the formula for calculating the internal rate of return (IRR)?

A. $NPV = 0$

B. $ROI = 100\%$

C. $NPV \times ROI$

D. $ROI \times NPV$

Answer: A

The internal rate of return (IRR) is the discount rate that makes the net present value (NPV) of all cash flows equal to zero.

➡18. What is the formula for calculating the price per square foot?

A. Total Price / Total Square Footage

B. Total Square Footage / Total Price

C. Total Price × Total Square Footage

D. Total Square Footage × Total Price

Answer: A.

The price per square foot is calculated by dividing the total price by the total square footage.

➡19. What is the formula for calculating the amortization schedule?

A. $P \times (r(1+r)^n) / ((1+r)^n-1)$

B. $P \times r \times n$

C. $P / r \times n$

D. $P \times n / r$

Answer: A

The formula for calculating the amortization schedule is $P \times (r(1+r)^n) / ((1+r)^n-1)$.

➡20. What is the formula for calculating the future value of an investment?

A. $P \times (1 + r)^n$

B. $P \times (1 - r)^n$

C. $P / (1 + r)^n$

D. $P / (1 - r)^n$

Answer: A

The future value of an investment is calculated as $P \times (1 + r)^n$.

➡21. How do you calculate the Net Operating Income (NOI) for a property?

A. Gross Income - Operating Expenses

B. Gross Income + Operating Expenses

C. Operating Expenses - Gross Income

D. Gross Income $\times$ Operating Expenses

Answer: A

Net Operating Income is calculated by subtracting the operating expenses from the gross income.

➡22. What is the formula for calculating the loan-to-value ratio (LTV)?

A. Mortgage Amount / Appraised Value

B. Appraised Value / Mortgage Amount

C. Mortgage Amount × Appraised Value

D. Appraised Value × Mortgage Amount

Answer: A

The loan-to-value ratio (LTV) is calculated by dividing the mortgage amount by the appraised value of the property.

➡**23. What is the formula for calculating the cash-on-cash return?**

A. Annual Pre-tax Cash Flow / Total Cash Invested

B. Total Cash Invested / Annual Pre-tax Cash Flow

C. Annual Pre-tax Cash Flow × Total Cash Invested

D. Total Cash Invested × Annual Pre-tax Cash Flow

Answer: A

The cash-on-cash return is calculated by dividing the annual pre-tax cash flow by the total cash invested.

➡**24. What is the formula for calculating the debt service coverage ratio (DSCR)?**

A. Net Operating Income / Debt Service

B. Debt Service / Net Operating Income

C. Net Operating Income × Debt Service

D. Debt Service × Net Operating Income

Answer: A

The debt service coverage ratio (DSCR) is calculated by dividing the net operating income by the debt service.

➡**25. What is the formula for calculating the equity build-up rate?**

A. (Principal Paid in Year 1 / Initial Investment) × 100

B. (Initial Investment / Principal Paid in Year 1) × 100

C. Principal Paid in Year 1 × Initial Investment

D. Initial Investment × Principal Paid in Year 1

Answer: A

The equity build-up rate is calculated by dividing the principal paid in the first year by the initial investment and then multiplying by 100.

➡26. What is the formula for calculating the gross operating income (GOI)?

A. Gross Potential Income - Vacancy and Credit Losses

B. Vacancy and Credit Losses - Gross Potential Income

C. Gross Potential Income × Vacancy and Credit Losses

D. Vacancy and Credit Losses × Gross Potential Income

Answer: A

The gross operating income (GOI) is calculated by subtracting vacancy and credit losses from the gross potential income.

➡27. What is the formula for calculating the effective gross income (EGI)?

A. Gross Operating Income + Other Income

B. Other Income - Gross Operating Income

C. Gross Operating Income × Other Income

D. Other Income × Gross Operating Income

Answer: A

The effective gross income (EGI) is calculated by adding other income to the gross operating income.

➡28. What is the formula for calculating the absorption rate?

A. Number of Units Sold / Number of Units Available

B. Number of Units Available / Number of Units Sold

C. Number of Units Sold × Number of Units Available

D. Number of Units Available × Number of Units Sold

Answer: A

The absorption rate is calculated by dividing the number of units sold by the number of units available.

➡**29. What is the formula for calculating the price-to-rent ratio?**

A. Home Price / Annual Rent

B. Annual Rent / Home Price

C. Home Price × Annual Rent

D. Annual Rent × Home Price

Answer: A

The price-to-rent ratio is calculated by dividing the home price by the annual rent.

➡**30. What is the formula for calculating the yield?**

A. Annual Income / Investment Cost

B. Investment Cost / Annual Income

C. Annual Income × Investment Cost

D. Investment Cost × Annual Income

Answer: A

The yield is calculated by dividing the annual income by the investment cost.

➡**31. What is the formula for calculating the Gross Rent Multiplier (GRM)?**

A. Sales Price / Monthly Rent

B. Monthly Rent / Sales Price

C. Sales Price × Monthly Rent

D. Monthly Rent × Sales Price

Answer: A

The Gross Rent Multiplier (GRM) is calculated by dividing the sales price by the monthly rent.

➡32. How do you calculate the Loan-to-Value ratio (LTV)?

A. Loan Amount / Appraised Value

B. Appraised Value / Loan Amount

C. Loan Amount × Appraised Value

D. Appraised Value × Loan Amount

Answer: A

The Loan-to-Value ratio (LTV) is calculated by dividing the loan amount by the appraised value of the property.

➡33. How do you calculate the Net Operating Income (NOI)?

A. Gross Operating Income - Operating Expenses

B. Operating Expenses - Gross Operating Income

C. Gross Operating Income × Operating Expenses

D. Operating Expenses × Gross Operating Income

Answer: A

The Net Operating Income (NOI) is calculated by subtracting the operating expenses from the gross operating income.

➡34. How do you calculate the Debt Service Coverage Ratio (DSCR)?

A. Net Operating Income / Debt Service

B. Debt Service / Net Operating Income

C. Net Operating Income × Debt Service

D. Debt Service × Net Operating Income

Answer: A

The Debt Service Coverage Ratio (DSCR) is calculated by dividing the Net Operating Income by the Debt Service.

➡35. What is the formula for calculating the Break-Even Ratio (BER)?

A. (Operating Expenses + Debt Service) / Gross Operating Income

B. Gross Operating Income / (Operating Expenses + Debt Service)

C. (Operating Expenses + Debt Service) × Gross Operating Income

D. Gross Operating Income × (Operating Expenses + Debt Service)

Answer: A

The Break-Even Ratio (BER) is calculated by dividing the sum of operating expenses and debt service by the gross operating income.

➡36. How do you calculate the Effective Gross Income (EGI)?

A. Gross Income - Vacancy Losses + Other Income

B. Gross Income + Vacancy Losses - Other Income

C. Gross Income × Vacancy Losses + Other Income

D. Gross Income + Vacancy Losses × Other Income

Answer: A

The Effective Gross Income (EGI) is calculated by subtracting vacancy losses from the gross income and adding any other income.

➡37. What is the formula for calculating the Operating Expense Ratio (OER)?

A. Operating Expenses / Effective Gross Income

B. Effective Gross Income / Operating Expenses

C. Operating Expenses × Effective Gross Income

D. Effective Gross Income × Operating Expenses

Answer: A

The Operating Expense Ratio (OER) is calculated by dividing the operating expenses by the effective gross income.

➡**38. How do you calculate the Cash-on-Cash Return?**

A. Cash Flow Before Taxes / Initial Investment

B. Initial Investment / Cash Flow Before Taxes

C. Cash Flow Before Taxes × Initial Investment

D. Initial Investment × Cash Flow Before Taxes

Answer: A

The Cash-on-Cash Return is calculated by dividing the cash flow before taxes by the initial investment.

➡**39. What is the formula for calculating the Amortization Factor?**

A. Monthly Payment / Loan Amount

B. Loan Amount / Monthly Payment

C. Monthly Payment × Loan Amount

D. Loan Amount × Monthly Payment

Answer: A

The Amortization Factor is calculated by dividing the monthly payment by the loan amount.

➡**40. How do you calculate the Equity Dividend Rate (EDR)?**

A. Cash Flow After Taxes / Equity Investment

B. Equity Investment / Cash Flow After Taxes

C. Cash Flow After Taxes × Equity Investment

D. Equity Investment × Cash Flow After Taxes

➡41. What is the formula for calculating the Debt Service Coverage Ratio (DSCR)?

A. Net Operating Income / Debt Service

B. Debt Service / Net Operating Income

C. Net Operating Income × Debt Service

D. Debt Service - Net Operating Income

Answer: A

The Debt Service Coverage Ratio is calculated by dividing the Net Operating Income by the Debt Service.

➡42. How do you calculate the Gross Rent Multiplier (GRM)?

A. Property Price / Monthly Rent

B. Monthly Rent / Property Price

C. Annual Rent / Property Price

D. Property Price / Annual Rent

Answer: A

The Gross Rent Multiplier is calculated by dividing the property price by the monthly rent.

➡43. What is the formula for calculating Loan-to-Value ratio?

A. Loan Amount / Property Value

B. Property Value / Loan Amount

C. Loan Amount × Property Value

D. Property Value - Loan Amount

Answer: A

The Loan-to-Value ratio is calculated by dividing the loan amount by the property value.

➡ **44. How do you calculate the break-even point in a real estate investment?**

    A. Fixed Costs / (Selling Price - Variable Costs)

    B. (Selling Price - Variable Costs) / Fixed Costs

    C. Fixed Costs × Selling Price

    D. Selling Price / Fixed Costs

Answer: A

The break-even point is calculated by dividing the fixed costs by the difference between the selling price and variable costs.

➡ **45. How do you calculate the Return on Investment (ROI) for a property?**

    A. (Net Profit / Investment Cost) × 100

    B. (Investment Cost / Net Profit) × 100

    C. Net Profit × Investment Cost

    D. Investment Cost - Net Profit

Answer: A

The Return on Investment is calculated by dividing the net profit by the investment cost and then multiplying by 100.

➡ **46. How do you calculate the equity in a property?**

    A. Property Value - Mortgage Balance

    B. Mortgage Balance - Property Value

    C. Property Value × Mortgage Balance

    D. Mortgage Balance / Property Value

Answer: A

Equity is calculated by subtracting the mortgage balance from the property value.

➡️47. What is the formula for calculating the amortization payment?

    A. Principal Amount / Number of Payments

    B. Interest Rate / Number of Payments

    C. (Principal Amount × Interest Rate) / Number of Payments

    D. (Principal Amount × Interest Rate) / (1 - (1 + Interest Rate)^-Number of Payments)

Answer: D

The amortization payment is calculated using the formula mentioned.

➡️48. What is the formula for calculating the Internal Rate of Return (IRR) for a real estate investment?

    A. The discount rate that makes the Net Present Value zero

    B. The rate that equals the Net Operating Income

    C. The rate that equals the Debt Service

    D. The rate that makes the Gross Income zero

Answer: A

The Internal Rate of Return is the discount rate that makes the Net Present Value of all cash flows from a particular investment equal to zero.

➡️49. What is the formula for calculating the rate of return on an investment property?

    A. (Net Profit / Cost of Investment) × 100

    B. (Cost of Investment / Net Profit) × 100

    C. Net Profit × Cost of Investment

D. Cost of Investment - Net Profit

Answer: A

The rate of return is calculated by dividing the net profit by the cost of the investment and then multiplying by 100.

➡ 50. How do you calculate the net profit from a real estate investment?

  A. Selling Price - (Buying Price + Costs)

  B. (Buying Price + Costs) - Selling Price

  C. Selling Price × Buying Price

  D. Buying Price / Selling Price

Answer: A

The Net Operating Income (NOI) is calculated by subtracting the operating expenses from the gross operating income.

Specialty Areas

The real estate industry is vast and diverse, offering various specialty areas that professionals can focus on. Whether you're a seasoned agent or a newcomer to the New Jersey real estate market, understanding these specialty areas can provide you with valuable insights and opportunities for career growth. This chapter will delve into the different specialty areas in New Jersey real estate, discussing their unique characteristics, requirements, and market trends.

Residential Real Estate

Single-Family Homes

This is the most common type of residential real estate. Agents specializing in this area focus on helping families find homes that meet their needs, from starter homes to luxury estates.

Condominiums and Townhouses

These properties offer a different lifestyle compared to single-family homes. They are generally part of larger complexes with shared amenities.

Vacation Homes

New Jersey, with its beautiful shorelines, is a popular location for vacation homes. Agents in this area often deal with seasonal rentals and property management.

Commercial Real Estate

Office Spaces

Agents specializing in office spaces work with businesses to find suitable locations for their operations, considering factors like location, size, and amenities.

Retail Spaces

This involves properties like shopping centers, standalone shops, and malls. Agents must understand consumer behavior and zoning laws.

Industrial Real Estate

This includes warehouses, factories, and other industrial facilities. Agents need to be knowledgeable about logistics and local manufacturing regulations.

Investment Real Estate

Rental Properties

Investing in rental properties can be lucrative but requires an understanding of property management and tenant laws.

Real Estate Investment Trusts (REITs)

These are companies that own or finance income-producing real estate across various sectors. They offer a way to invest in real estate without owning physical property.

Flipping Properties

This involves buying properties, improving them, and selling them for a profit. It's a high-risk, high-reward area that requires a deep understanding of the local market.

Luxury Real Estate

Agents in this area deal with high-end properties, often worth millions of dollars. They need to understand the unique needs and expectations of affluent clients.

Farm and Land

Agricultural Real Estate

This involves properties used for farming and other agricultural activities. Agents must be familiar with land use regulations and agricultural practices.

Undeveloped Land

This includes vacant land that can be used for various purposes, from residential to commercial development.

Historic Homes

New Jersey has a rich history, and many agents specialize in historic homes. These agents must understand the specific regulations and challenges associated with these properties.

Foreclosures and Short Sales

Agents specializing in this area help buyers find properties that are being sold by lenders or are in the process of foreclosure.

Green and Sustainable Real Estate

This is an emerging field focusing on eco-friendly and sustainable properties. Agents need to be knowledgeable about green technologies and sustainability practices.

Niche Markets

Senior Living

Agents in this area focus on properties suitable for seniors, such as retirement communities and assisted living facilities.

Student Housing

With several universities in New Jersey, student housing is a significant market. Agents must understand the needs and limitations of student renters.

Legal and Ethical Considerations

Each specialty area comes with its own set of legal and ethical considerations. For example, agents dealing with commercial properties need to understand commercial leasing laws, while those in residential real estate must be well-versed in fair housing laws.

Conclusion

Specializing in a particular area of real estate can provide agents with a competitive edge. It allows them to offer expert advice and tailored services to their clients. Whether you're interested in residential, commercial, or investment properties, understanding the various specialty areas in New Jersey real estate will equip you with the knowledge and skills needed to excel in this dynamic industry.

Mock Exam Specialty Areas

➡ 1. Which type of real estate is often the entry point for many new agents and brokers?

    A. Commercial

    B. Industrial

    C. Residential

    D. Luxury

Answer: C. Residential

Explanation: The chapter states that residential real estate is often the entry point for many new agents and brokers.

➡ 2. What type of property is a penthouse?

    A. Industrial

    B. Commercial

    C. Residential

    D. Luxury

Answer: D. Luxury

Explanation: Penthouses are high-end apartments located on the top floors of high-rise buildings and fall under luxury real estate.

➡ 3. What is a key skill required in commercial real estate?

    A. Financial Analysis

    B. Knowledge of Industrial Machinery

    C. Strong Interpersonal Skills

    D. Discretion and Confidentiality

Answer: A. Financial Analysis

Explanation: Financial analysis is crucial in commercial real estate for understanding balance sheets, income statements, and cash flow.

➡ 4. What type of property is a factory?

A. Commercial

B. Industrial

C. Residential

D. Luxury

Answer: B. Industrial

Explanation: Factories are geared towards manufacturing, production, and distribution, which falls under industrial real estate.

➡ 5. What is a key regulatory aspect in industrial real estate?

A. Luxury tax implications

B. OSHA regulations

C. Fair Housing Laws

D. Commercial zoning laws

Answer: B. OSHA regulations

Explanation: Occupational Safety and Health Administration (OSHA) regulations are key in industrial real estate.

➡ 6. What type of property is a shopping mall?

A. Commercial

B. Industrial

C. Residential

D. Luxury

Answer: A. Commercial

Explanation: Shopping malls fall under commercial real estate as they are used for business activities.

➡7. What is a key skill required in luxury real estate?

A. Financial Analysis

B. Knowledge of Industrial Machinery

C. Strong Interpersonal Skills

D. Discretion and Confidentiality

Answer: D. Discretion and Confidentiality

Explanation: Clients in the luxury sector value their privacy highly, making discretion and confidentiality key skills.

➡8. What type of property is a townhouse?

A. Commercial

B. Industrial

C. Residential

D. Luxury

Answer: C. Residential

Explanation: Townhouses are multi-floor homes designed for individual or family living, which falls under residential real estate.

➡9. What is a key regulatory aspect in residential real estate?

A. Luxury tax implications

B. OSHA regulations

C. Fair Housing Laws

D. Commercial zoning laws

Answer: C. Fair Housing Laws

Explanation: Fair Housing Laws are key regulatory aspects in residential real estate to ensure equal opportunity in housing.

➡10. What type of property is a distribution center?

A. Commercial

B. Industrial

C. Residential

D. Luxury

Answer: B. Industrial

Explanation: Distribution centers are used for storing and distributing goods, which falls under industrial real estate.

➡11. What type of real estate involves the sale of businesses?

A. Commercial

B. Business Brokerage

C. Residential

D. Luxury

Answer: B. Business Brokerage

Explanation: Business Brokerage involves the sale of businesses, including their assets and real estate.

➡12. What is a key skill required in business brokerage?

A. Negotiation Skills

B. Knowledge of Industrial Machinery

C. Strong Interpersonal Skills

D. Financial Analysis

Answer: A. Negotiation Skills

Explanation: Negotiation skills are crucial in business brokerage to secure the best deals for clients.

➡ 13. What type of real estate involves the sale of farmland?

A. Commercial

B. Industrial

C. Agricultural

D. Luxury

Answer: C. Agricultural

Explanation: Agricultural real estate involves the sale of farmland and agricultural facilities.

➡ 14. What is a key regulatory aspect in agricultural real estate?

A. EPA Regulations

B. OSHA regulations

C. Fair Housing Laws

D. Luxury tax implications

Answer: A. EPA Regulations

Explanation: Environmental Protection Agency (EPA) regulations are key in agricultural real estate.

15. What type of property is a hotel?

A. Commercial

B. Industrial

C. Residential

D. Hospitality

Answer: D. Hospitality

Explanation: Hotels fall under hospitality real estate, which is a sub-category of commercial real estate.

16. What is a key skill required in hospitality real estate?

A. Customer Service

B. Knowledge of Industrial Machinery

C. Strong Interpersonal Skills

D. Financial Analysis

Answer: A. Customer Service

Explanation: Customer service is crucial in hospitality real estate to ensure guest satisfaction.

17. What type of real estate involves the sale of undeveloped land?

A. Commercial

B. Land

C. Residential

D. Luxury

Answer: B. Land

Explanation: The sale of undeveloped land falls under land real estate.

18. What is a key regulatory aspect in land real estate?

A. Zoning Laws

B. OSHA regulations

C. Fair Housing Laws

D. Luxury tax implications

Answer: A. Zoning Laws

Explanation: Zoning laws are key in land real estate to determine the types of development that can occur.

➡19. What type of property is a condominium?

A. Commercial

B. Industrial

C. Residential

D. Luxury

Answer: C. Residential

Explanation: Condominiums are multi-unit properties that are sold individually, which falls under residential real estate.

➡20. What is a key skill required in land real estate?

A. Negotiation Skills

B. Knowledge of Zoning Laws

C. Strong Interpersonal Skills

D. Financial Analysis

Answer: B. Knowledge of Zoning Laws

Explanation: Knowledge of zoning laws is crucial in land real estate to guide clients on permissible uses.

➡21. What is the primary focus of industrial real estate?

A. Warehouses

B. Hotels

C. Farmland

D. Condominiums

Answer: A. Warehouses

Explanation: Industrial real estate primarily focuses on warehouses and manufacturing buildings.

➡22. What is a 1031 exchange commonly used for?

A. Residential properties

B. Commercial properties

C. Agricultural properties

D. Industrial properties

Answer: B. Commercial properties

Explanation: A 1031 exchange is commonly used to defer capital gains tax in commercial real estate.

➡23. What is the main consideration in retail real estate?

A. Location

B. Size

C. Zoning

D. Tax implications

Answer: A. Location

Explanation: Location is the main consideration in retail real estate, as it directly impacts customer footfall.

24. What is the primary focus of residential real estate?

A. Single-family homes

B. Warehouses

C. Hotels

D. Farmland

Answer: A. Single-family homes

Explanation: Residential real estate primarily focuses on single-family homes, although it can include multi-family units.

25. What is the main consideration in luxury real estate?

A. Price

B. Location

C. Amenities

D. Size

Answer: C. Amenities

Explanation: Luxury real estate often focuses on the amenities offered, such as pools, gyms, and concierge services.

26. What is the primary advantage of investing in mixed-use real estate?

A. Diversification

B. Lower taxes

C. Easier management

D. Higher rent

Answer: A. Diversification

Explanation: Mixed-use real estate offers diversification as it combines residential, commercial, and sometimes industrial spaces.

➡27. What is the main disadvantage of investing in vacation real estate?

A. Seasonal income

B. High maintenance

C. Zoning restrictions

D. High taxes

Answer: A. Seasonal income

Explanation: Vacation real estate often has seasonal income, which can be a disadvantage for consistent cash flow.

➡28. What is the primary consideration when investing in student housing?

A. Proximity to educational institutions

B. Luxury amenities

C. Tax benefits

D. Size of the property

Answer: A. Proximity to educational institutions

Explanation: The primary consideration for student housing is its proximity to educational institutions.

➡29. What is the main benefit of investing in senior living communities?

A. Lower maintenance

B. Steady income

C. Tax benefits

D. High rent

Answer: B. Steady income

Explanation: Senior living communities often provide a steady income due to long-term leases.

→30. What is a triple net lease commonly used in?

A. Residential properties

B. Commercial properties

C. Industrial properties

D. Agricultural properties

Answer: B. Commercial properties

Explanation: A triple net lease is commonly used in commercial real estate, where the tenant pays property taxes, insurance, and maintenance costs.

→31. What is the primary focus of hospitality real estate?

A. Hotels and resorts

B. Warehouses

C. Office buildings

D. Farmland

Answer: A. Hotels and resorts

Explanation: Hospitality real estate primarily focuses on hotels, resorts, and other lodging options.

→32. What is the main consideration in agricultural real estate?

A. Soil quality

B. Location

C. Size

D. Zoning

Answer: A. Soil quality

Explanation: Soil quality is the main consideration in agricultural real estate for farming purposes.

→33. What is the primary advantage of investing in REITs?

A. Liquidity

B. Control over property

C. Tax benefits

D. High rent

Answer: A. Liquidity

Explanation: REITs offer liquidity as they can be easily bought and sold on stock exchanges.

→34. What is the main disadvantage of investing in office real estate?

A. High vacancy rates

B. Seasonal income

C. Zoning restrictions

D. High maintenance

Answer: A. High vacancy rates

Explanation: Office real estate can have high vacancy rates, especially in economic downturns.

→35. What is the primary focus of mobile home parks?

A. Affordable housing

B. Luxury living

C. Commercial spaces

D. Agricultural land

Answer: A. Affordable housing

Explanation: Mobile home parks primarily focus on providing affordable housing options.

➡36. What is the primary consideration when investing in retail real estate?

A. Foot traffic

B. Tax benefits

C. Size of the property

D. Proximity to educational institutions

Answer: A. Foot traffic

Explanation: Foot traffic is crucial for the success of retail real estate.

➡37. What is the main benefit of investing in industrial real estate?

A. High rent

B. Long-term leases

C. Seasonal income

D. Tax benefits

Answer: B. Long-term leases

Explanation: Industrial real estate often comes with long-term leases, providing stable income.

➡38. What is a common disadvantage of investing in multi-family properties?

A. High maintenance costs

B. Low rent

C. Zoning restrictions

D. Seasonal income

Answer: A. High maintenance costs

Explanation: Multi-family properties often have higher maintenance costs due to multiple units.

39. What is the primary focus of medical real estate?

A. Hospitals and clinics

B. Office buildings

C. Warehouses

D. Hotels and resorts

Answer: A. Hospitals and clinics

Explanation: Medical real estate primarily focuses on hospitals, clinics, and other healthcare facilities.

40. What is the main consideration in raw land investment?

A. Zoning restrictions

B. Soil quality

C. Location

D. Size

Answer: C. Location

Explanation: Location is key in raw land investment for future development.

41. What is the primary advantage of investing in storage units?

A. Low maintenance

B. High rent

C. Tax benefits

D. Seasonal income

Answer: A. Low maintenance

Explanation: Storage units generally require low maintenance.

➡42. What is the main disadvantage of investing in co-working spaces?

A. High vacancy rates

B. Low rent

C. Zoning restrictions

D. Seasonal income

Answer: A. High vacancy rates

Explanation: Co-working spaces can have high vacancy rates, especially during economic downturns.

➡43. What is the primary focus of green real estate?

A. Energy efficiency

B. High rent

C. Tax benefits

D. Size of the property

Answer: A. Energy efficiency

Explanation: Green real estate primarily focuses on energy efficient buildings.

➡44. What is the main benefit of investing in brownfield sites?

A. Tax incentives

B. High rent

C. Seasonal income

D. Long-term leases

Answer: A. Tax incentives

Explanation: Brownfield sites often come with tax incentives for redevelopment.

➡️45. What is the primary consideration when investing in infill real estate?

A. Location

B. Size

C. Zoning restrictions

D. Soil quality

Answer: A. Location

Explanation: Infill real estate focuses on developing vacant or underused parcels within existing urban areas, so location is key.

➡️46. What is the main disadvantage of investing in luxury real estate?

A. High maintenance costs

B. Seasonal income

C. Zoning restrictions

D. Low rent

Answer: A. High maintenance costs

Explanation: Luxury real estate often comes with high maintenance costs.

➡️47. What is the primary focus of transit-oriented development?

A. Proximity to public transport

B. Luxury amenities

C. Tax benefits

D. Size of the property

Answer: A. Proximity to public transport

Explanation: Transit-oriented development focuses on properties close to public transport facilities.

→48. What is the main benefit of investing in adaptive reuse properties?

A. Tax incentives

B. High rent

C. Seasonal income

D. Long-term leases

Answer: A. Tax incentives

Explanation: Adaptive reuse properties often come with tax incentives for redevelopment.

→49. What is the primary consideration when investing in distressed properties?

A. Cost of renovation

B. Location

C. Size

D. Zoning

Answer: A. Cost of renovation

Explanation: The cost of renovation is a key consideration when investing in distressed properties.

→50. What is the main disadvantage of investing in fixer-uppers?

A. High renovation costs

B. Low rent

C. Zoning restrictions

D. Seasonal income

Answer: A. High renovation costs

Explanation: Fixer-uppers often come with high renovation costs that can eat into profits.

Ethics and Legal Considerations

Ethics and legal considerations are the backbone of any profession, and the real estate industry is no exception. In New Jersey, real estate professionals are bound by both state laws and ethical guidelines to ensure that they conduct business in a manner that is legal, ethical, and beneficial for all parties involved. This chapter aims to provide an in-depth look at the ethical and legal considerations that real estate professionals in New Jersey should be aware of.

Ethical Guidelines

Code of Ethics

The National Association of Realtors (NAR) provides a Code of Ethics that serves as the industry standard for ethical conduct. This code is adopted by various state and local real estate associations, including those in New Jersey.

Fiduciary Duties

Real estate agents have a fiduciary duty to their clients, which means they must act in the best interests of their clients at all times. This includes confidentiality, full disclosure, and the duty to avoid conflicts of interest.

Honesty and Integrity

Agents are expected to conduct all business with honesty and integrity. This includes not misleading clients or providing false information.

Legal Considerations

Licensing Laws

In New Jersey, all real estate agents must be licensed by the New Jersey Real Estate Commission. This involves passing a state exam and meeting other eligibility criteria.

Contract Laws

Contracts are a fundamental part of real estate transactions. Agents must understand the elements of a legally binding contract, including offer, acceptance, and consideration.

Fair Housing Laws

The Fair Housing Act prohibits discrimination based on race, color, religion, sex, disability, familial status, or national origin. New Jersey has its own set of fair housing laws that provide additional protections.

Disclosure Requirements

New Jersey law requires sellers to provide a disclosure statement that outlines the condition of the property. Failure to disclose known defects could result in legal consequences.

Common Legal Issues

Dual Agency

Dual agency occurs when a real estate agent represents both the buyer and the seller in a transaction. This can create a conflict of interest, and full disclosure is required.

Escrow and Trust Funds

Agents are responsible for handling escrow and trust funds correctly. Mismanagement of these funds can result in severe legal consequences.

Zoning and Land Use

Agents should be familiar with local zoning laws and land use regulations, as these can significantly impact a property's value and intended use.

Risk Management

Professional Liability Insurance

Also known as Errors and Omissions (E&O) insurance, this protects agents from legal claims or disputes.

Record-Keeping

Proper record-keeping can help protect against legal issues. This includes keeping copies of all contracts, correspondence, and other transaction-related documents.

Continuing Education

Many legal issues can be avoided through proper education. New Jersey requires real estate agents to complete continuing education courses as part of their license renewal process.

Case Studies

Case Study 1: Fair Housing Violation

An agent in New Jersey was found guilty of steering minority clients away from certain neighborhoods. This is a violation of both the NAR Code of Ethics and federal and state fair housing laws.

Case Study 2: Failure to Disclose

An agent failed to disclose known issues with a property's foundation. The buyers sued the agent for misrepresentation and won.

Conclusion

Ethics and legal considerations are not just guidelines but are crucial for the long-term success and reputation of a real estate professional. Understanding and adhering to ethical principles and legal requirements not only protect agents from legal repercussions but also ensure that they provide the best service to their clients. In New Jersey, where the real estate market is both competitive and regulated, being well-versed in these areas is not just an option but a necessity.

Mock Exam Ethics and Legal Considerations

➡1. What are the three main categories of the NAR Code of Ethics?

A. Duties to Clients, Duties to Realtors, Duties to the Public

B. Duties to Clients and Customers, Duties to the Public, Duties to Realtors

C. Duties to Sellers, Duties to Buyers, Duties to the Public

D. Duties to the Government, Duties to Clients, Duties to Realtors

Answer: B

The NAR Code of Ethics is divided into three main categories: Duties to Clients and Customers, Duties to the Public, and Duties to Realtors.

➡2. Which of the following is NOT a fiduciary duty?

A. Loyalty

B. Confidentiality

C. Manipulation

D. Full Disclosure

Answer: C

Manipulation is not a fiduciary duty. The fiduciary duties are loyalty, confidentiality, obedience, reasonable care, accounting, and full disclosure.

➡3. What is the primary purpose of zoning laws?

A. To increase property taxes

B. To regulate land use

C. To protect endangered species

D. To promote business

Answer: B

The primary purpose of zoning laws is to regulate land use, such as residential, commercial, or industrial zones.

➡4. What does 'reasonable care' in fiduciary duties imply?

    A. Taking vacations regularly

    B. Staying updated on market trends

    C. Investing in real estate

    D. Focusing on commission

Answer: B

'Reasonable care' means staying updated on market trends, legal changes, and other factors that could affect a client's decision.

➡5. What is the consequence of not adhering to full disclosure?

    A. Increased commission

    B. Legal repercussions

    C. More clients

    D. Promotion

Answer: B

Failing to adhere to full disclosure can lead to legal repercussions, including lawsuits and loss of license.

➡6. Which federal law is designed to ensure fair housing?

    A. The Sherman Act

    B. The Fair Housing Act

    C. The Clayton Act

    D. The Dodd-Frank Act

Answer: B

The Fair Housing Act is designed to prevent discrimination in housing based on race, color, religion, sex, or national origin.

➡7. What is the minimum age requirement for obtaining a real estate license in most states?

A. 16

B. 18

C. 21

D. 25

Answer: B

The minimum age requirement for obtaining a real estate license in most states is 18 years.

➡8. What is the key to resolving ethical dilemmas like dual agency?

A. Ignoring the issue

B. Full disclosure and informed consent

C. Choosing one party to represent

D. Consulting a lawyer

Answer: B

The key to resolving ethical dilemmas like dual agency lies in full disclosure and obtaining informed consent from all parties involved.

➡9. Which of the following is NOT an element that makes a contract legally binding?

A. Offer and acceptance

B. Consideration

C. Coercion

D. Legality of purpose

Answer: C

Coercion is not an element that makes a contract legally binding. A contract must have offer and acceptance, consideration, and legality of purpose to be legally binding.

➡**10. What does the NAR Code of Ethics say about advertising?**

A. It encourages aggressive advertising

B. It prohibits all forms of advertising

C. It requires truthful advertising

D. It promotes online advertising only

Answer: C

The NAR Code of Ethics requires that all advertising be truthful and not misleading.

➡**11. What is the primary role of the Real Estate Commission in most states?**

A. To sell properties

B. To regulate and license real estate agents

C. To build homes

D. To provide loans

Answer: B

The primary role of the Real Estate Commission in most states is to regulate and license real estate agents.

➡**12. What is the statute of frauds?**

A. A law that requires certain contracts to be in writing

B. A law that allows fraud in certain cases

C. A law that regulates online advertising

D. A law that deals with zoning issues

Answer: A

The statute of frauds is a law that requires certain contracts, like those for the sale of real estate, to be in writing to be enforceable.

➡13. What does RESPA stand for?

A. Real Estate Settlement Procedures Act

B. Real Estate Sales Professional Act

C. Residential Sales Property Act

D. Real Estate Security Policy Act

Answer: A

RESPA stands for Real Estate Settlement Procedures Act, which aims to provide transparency in the home buying process.

➡14. What is puffing in real estate terms?

A. Illegal misrepresentation

B. Exaggeration of property features

C. Accurate description of property

D. Undervaluing a property

Answer: B

Puffing refers to the exaggeration of property features, which is generally considered legal but can be ethically questionable.

➡15. What is the primary purpose of an escrow account?

A. To hold funds for investment

B. To hold funds until the completion of a real estate transaction

C. To pay for the agent's commission

D. To pay property taxes

Answer: B

The primary purpose of an escrow account is to hold funds until the completion of a real estate transaction.

➡16. What does the term "redlining" refer to?

A. Drawing property boundaries

B. Discriminatory lending practices

C. Marking properties for demolition

D. Highlighting important clauses in a contract

Answer: B

Redlining refers to discriminatory lending practices that deny loans or insurance to people based on their location, often targeting minority communities.

➡17. What is the difference between ethics and laws?

A. Ethics are legally binding, laws are not

B. Laws are legally binding, ethics are not

C. Ethics and laws are the same

D. Laws are optional, ethics are mandatory

Answer: B

Laws are legally binding rules that must be followed, while ethics are moral principles that guide behavior but are not legally enforceable.

➡18. What is the "doctrine of caveat emptor"?

A. Let the buyer beware

B. Let the seller beware

C. Buyer's premium

D. Seller's advantage

Answer: A

The doctrine of "caveat emptor" means "let the buyer beware," indicating that the buyer is responsible for due diligence.

➡19. What is a bilateral contract?

A. A contract with only one party

B. A contract with two parties

C. A contract with multiple parties

D. A contract that is not legally binding

Answer: B

A bilateral contract is a contract involving two parties where each party has made a promise to the other.

➡20. What is the role of a title company?

A. To market properties

B. To ensure the title is clear and prepare for its transfer

C. To provide loans

D. To build homes

Answer: B

The role of a title company is to ensure that the title to a piece of real estate is legitimate and to prepare for its transfer from the seller to the buyer.

➡21. What is the "dual agency" in real estate?

A. When an agent represents both the buyer and the seller

B. When two agents work for the same client

C. When an agent works for two different real estate firms

D. When an agent sells both commercial and residential properties

Answer: A

Dual agency occurs when a real estate agent represents both the buyer and the seller in the same transaction.

➡22. What does the Fair Housing Act prohibit?

A. Discrimination based on race, color, religion, sex, or national origin

B. All forms of discrimination

C. Discrimination based on financial status

D. Discrimination based on occupation

Answer: A

The Fair Housing Act prohibits discrimination in housing based on race, color, religion, sex, or national origin.

➡23. What is earnest money?

A. Money paid by the buyer at the time of the property closing

B. A refundable deposit

C. Money paid by the buyer to show serious intent to purchase

D. Money paid by the seller as a part of the listing agreement

Answer: C

Earnest money is money paid by the buyer to show serious intent to purchase the property.

➡24. What is a contingency in a real estate contract?

A. A binding clause

B. A non-negotiable term

C. A condition that must be met for the contract to be binding

D. A penalty for breach of contract

Answer: C

A contingency is a condition that must be met for the contract to be binding, such as a home inspection.

➡25. What is a fiduciary duty?

A. A legal obligation to act in the best interest of another

B. A duty to find the best property for a client

C. A duty to sell a property as quickly as possible

D. A duty to maximize profit

Answer: A

A fiduciary duty is a legal obligation to act in the best interest of another, such as a client.

➡26. What is a unilateral contract?

A. A contract where only one party makes a promise

B. A contract where both parties make promises

C. A contract that involves more than two parties

D. A contract that is not legally binding

Answer: A

A unilateral contract is a contract where only one party makes a promise, and the other has the option to complete the action.

➡️**27. What is the purpose of a disclosure statement?**

    A. To disclose the agent's commission

    B. To disclose any known defects or issues with the property

    C. To disclose the buyer's financial status

    D. To disclose the terms of the mortgage

Answer: B

The purpose of a disclosure statement is to disclose any known defects or issues with the property to the buyer.

➡️**28. What does "time is of the essence" mean in a real estate contract?**

    A. Deadlines must be strictly adhered to

    B. Time limits are flexible

    C. The contract has no expiration date

    D. The contract can be terminated at any time

Answer: A

"Time is of the essence" means that deadlines set forth in the contract must be strictly adhered to.

➡️**29. What is a quitclaim deed?**

    A. A deed that transfers property with no warranties

    B. A deed that includes warranties

    C. A deed that transfers leasehold interest

    D. A deed that can be easily revoked

Answer: A

A quitclaim deed is a deed that transfers property with no warranties or guarantees.

➡30. What is the role of a notary public in a real estate transaction?

A. To negotiate the terms

B. To verify the identity of the parties and witness the signing of documents

C. To provide legal advice

D. To inspect the property

Answer: B

The role of a notary public is to verify the identity of the parties and witness the signing of important documents.

➡31. What is the primary purpose of a title search?

A. To determine the property's market value

B. To verify the legal owner of the property

C. To inspect the condition of the property

D. To assess property taxes

Answer: B

The primary purpose of a title search is to verify the legal owner of the property and ensure there are no liens or other encumbrances.

➡32. What is a "balloon payment" in a mortgage?

A. A small initial payment

B. A large final payment

C. A regular monthly payment

D. An extra payment to reduce interest

Answer: B

A balloon payment is a large final payment at the end of a loan term, usually after a series of smaller payments.

➡️**33. What is the "right of first refusal" in real estate?**

A. The right to refuse a sale

B. The right to be the first to purchase a property before the owner sells it to another party

C. The right to refuse to pay rent

D. The right to refuse a home inspection

Answer: B

The right of first refusal allows an individual or entity the opportunity to purchase a property before the owner sells it to another party.

➡️**34. What is a "listing agreement"?**

A. An agreement between buyer and seller

B. An agreement between a seller and a real estate agent

C. An agreement between a buyer and a real estate agent

D. An agreement between two real estate agents

Answer: B

A listing agreement is a contract between a seller and a real estate agent outlining the terms under which the agent will sell the property.

➡️**35. What does "under contract" mean in real estate?**

A. The property is being appraised

B. The property is being inspected

C. An offer on the property has been accepted, but the sale is not yet complete

D. The property has been sold

Answer: C

"Under contract" means that an offer on the property has been accepted, but the sale is not yet complete, pending contingencies or other terms.

→ **36. What is the role of a fiduciary in a real estate transaction?**

  A. To act in the best interest of the client

  B. To maximize profits for the brokerage

  C. To represent both buyer and seller equally

  D. To ensure the property passes inspection

Answer: A

The role of a fiduciary is to act in the best interest of the client, whether that's the buyer or the seller.

→ **37. What does "escrow" refer to in real estate?**

  A. A type of mortgage loan

  B. A neutral third party holding funds or documents until conditions are met

  C. A binding contract between buyer and seller

  D. A home inspection report

Answer: B

Escrow refers to a neutral third party holding funds or documents until certain conditions are met in a real estate transaction.

→ **38. What is a "contingency" in a real estate contract?**

  A. A penalty for late payment

  B. A condition that must be met for the contract to proceed

  C. An optional add-on to the property

D. A mandatory fee paid to the real estate agent

Answer: B

A contingency is a condition that must be met for the contract to proceed, such as a successful home inspection.

➡39. What does "amortization" mean in the context of a mortgage?

A. The process of increasing the loan amount

B. The process of paying off the loan over time

C. The process of adjusting the interest rate

D. The process of transferring the loan to another lender

Answer: B

Amortization is the process of paying off a loan over time through regular payments.

➡40. What is "due diligence" in real estate?

A. The responsibility to investigate a property before purchase

B. The obligation to pay property taxes

C. The requirement to obtain a mortgage pre-approval

D. The duty to disclose all known defects to a buyer

Answer: A

Due diligence is the responsibility of the buyer to investigate a property thoroughly before completing the purchase.

➡41. What is "redlining" in the context of real estate?

A. Drawing property boundaries

B. Discriminatory practice affecting mortgage availability

C. A type of home inspection

D. A negotiation strategy

Answer: B

Redlining is a discriminatory practice where mortgage lenders deny loans or insurance to certain areas based on racial or ethnic composition.

➡ **42. What does "title insurance" protect against?**

A. Property damage

B. Mortgage default

C. Legal claims against property ownership

D. Loss of rental income

Answer: C

Title insurance protects against legal claims challenging the ownership of the property.

➡ **43. What is "dual agency" in real estate?**

A. When an agent represents both the buyer and the seller

B. When two agents from the same brokerage represent the buyer and the seller

C. When an agent represents two buyers for the same property

D. When an agent represents two sellers for different properties

Answer: A

Dual agency occurs when a real estate agent represents both the buyer and the seller in the same transaction. This can create a conflict of interest and is illegal in some states.

➡ **44. What is a "balloon mortgage"?**

A. A mortgage with fluctuating interest rates

B. A mortgage that requires a large final payment

C. A mortgage with no down payment

D. A mortgage paid off in less than 5 years

Answer: B

A balloon mortgage requires a large final payment at the end of the loan term.

➡️45. What is "blockbusting"?

A. Building multiple properties in a short time

B. Encouraging people to sell their homes by instigating fear of a changing neighborhood

C. The process of rezoning land

D. Buying large blocks of property for development

Answer: B

Blockbusting is the practice of encouraging people to sell their homes by instigating fear, often related to racial, ethnic, or social change in a neighborhood.

➡️46. What is a "1031 exchange"?

A. A tax-deferred property exchange

B. A type of mortgage loan

C. A property auction

D. An open house event

Answer: A

A 1031 exchange allows the owner to sell a property and reinvest the proceeds in a new property while deferring capital gains tax.

➡️47. What is "eminent domain"?

A. The right of the government to acquire private property for public use

B. The highest legal ownership of property

C. A type of zoning regulation

D. A clause in a mortgage contract

Answer: A

Eminent domain is the right of the government to acquire private property for public use, usually with compensation.

➡48. What is "equity" in real estate?

A. The market value of a property

B. The difference between the property's market value and the remaining mortgage balance

C. The initial down payment

D. The annual property tax

Answer: B

Equity is the difference between the market value of the property and the remaining balance on any loans secured by the property.

➡49. What is "escrow" in a real estate transaction?

A. A legal arrangement where a third party holds funds or documents

B. The initial offer made by a buyer

C. The final stage of mortgage approval

D. A type of home inspection

Answer: A

Escrow is a legal arrangement in which a third party temporarily holds funds or documents until the conditions of a contract are met.

➡50. What is "net operating income" in real estate investment?

A. Gross income minus operating expenses

B. Gross income plus operating expenses

C. Mortgage payments minus rental income

D. Property value minus mortgage balance

Answer: A

Net operating income is the gross income generated by a property minus the operating expenses, not including mortgage payments or taxes.

Day of the Exam

The day of the New Jersey Real Estate License Exam is a pivotal moment in your journey to becoming a licensed real estate professional. The preparation leading up to this day is crucial, but what you do on the actual day can make or break your chances of passing. This chapter aims to provide you with a comprehensive guide on what to expect and how to navigate the day of the exam successfully.

Pre-Exam Checklist

Documentation

Ensure you have all the necessary identification and authorization documents. Typically, you'll need a government-issued photo ID and your exam authorization letter.

Supplies

Bring at least two forms of ID, multiple pencils, and a calculator if allowed. Check the specific rules for your testing center.

Dress Code

Dress comfortably but professionally. Some testing centers have specific dress code requirements, so make sure to check beforehand.

Nutrition

Eat a balanced meal before leaving for the exam. Avoid excessive caffeine, as it can make you jittery and affect your concentration.

Arriving at the Testing Center

Timing

Aim to arrive at least 30 minutes before your scheduled exam time. This will give you ample time to check-in and get settled.

Check-In Process

Upon arrival, you'll go through a check-in process that includes verifying your identification and storing your belongings in a designated area.

Pre-Exam Briefing

Before the exam starts, a proctor will brief you on the rules and regulations, including time limits and permitted materials.

The Exam Room

Layout

The exam room will likely have individual workstations with computers for each candidate. Familiarize yourself with the layout as soon as you enter.

Technical Aspects

Make sure the computer and any other equipment are working correctly. If you encounter any issues, notify the proctor immediately.

Time Management

Keep an eye on the clock. The New Jersey Real Estate License Exam is time-limited, so managing your time effectively is crucial.

Taking the Exam

Reading Questions

Read each question carefully. Misinterpreting a question can lead to incorrect answers.

Answering Strategy

Answer the questions you are sure about first, then go back to the more challenging ones. This ensures that you don't run out of time while pondering over a single question.

Review

If time permits, review your answers before submitting the exam. Make sure you haven't left any questions unanswered unless you are penalized for guessing.

Post-Exam Procedures

Submitting the Exam

Once you've completed the exam, you'll submit it electronically through the computer system. Follow the proctor's instructions for this process.

Preliminary Results

In most cases, you'll receive preliminary results immediately after submitting the exam. These results will indicate whether you've passed or failed but are not considered official until validated.

Official Results

Your official results will usually be mailed to you within a few weeks. These results will include a breakdown of your performance in different subject areas.

Tips for Success

Stay Calm

Anxiety and stress can severely impact your performance. Take deep breaths and stay as calm as possible throughout the exam.

Trust Your Preparation

You've spent weeks or even months preparing for this day. Trust your preparation and your ability to succeed.

Be Mindful of Others

Remember that you're not the only one taking the exam. Be respectful and mindful of other examinees.

Conclusion

The day of the New Jersey Real Estate License Exam is undoubtedly stressful, but with the right preparation and mindset, you can navigate it successfully. From the moment you wake up to the moment you receive your results, every action you take can contribute to your success. This chapter has aimed to provide you with a detailed roadmap for the day, and we hope it serves you well as you take this significant step in your real estate career. Good luck!

After the Exam: Next Steps

Congratulations on completing the New Jersey Real Estate License Exam! Whether you've passed or are awaiting results, this chapter is designed to guide you through the crucial steps that come after the exam. From understanding your results to planning your career, we'll cover it all.

Understanding Your Results

Preliminary Results

Most testing centers provide preliminary results immediately after the exam. While these are not your official results, they give you a good indication of your performance.

Official Results

Your official results will be mailed to you within a few weeks. These results will include a detailed breakdown of your performance in each subject area, which can be useful for future reference or in case you need to retake the exam.

If You Passed

Celebrate

Take a moment to celebrate your achievement. Passing the real estate exam is a significant milestone, and you should be proud of yourself.

License Application

The next step is to apply for your real estate license. You'll need to fill out an application form, submit any required documents, and pay the licensing fee.

Background Check

Expect to undergo a background check as part of the licensing process. This is a standard procedure to ensure that you meet all the ethical and legal requirements to practice real estate in New Jersey.

Joining a Brokerage

As a newly licensed real estate agent, you'll need to join a brokerage to start practicing. Research different brokerages to find one that aligns with your career goals and offers the support you need.

MLS Access

Once you join a brokerage, you'll gain access to the Multiple Listing Service (MLS), a crucial tool for any real estate agent. The MLS provides comprehensive data on available properties, which you'll use daily in your work.

Continuing Education

Even after obtaining your license, your education shouldn't stop. Many states, including New Jersey, require real estate agents to complete continuing education courses to renew their licenses.

If You Didn't Pass

Don't Despair

Failing the exam can be disheartening, but it's not the end of the world. Many successful real estate agents didn't pass on their first try.

Review Your Weak Areas

Your official results will indicate where you performed poorly. Use this information to focus your study efforts for your next attempt.

Reapply for the Exam

You'll need to wait for a specified period before you can retake the exam. Use this time to prepare thoroughly, focusing on your weak areas.

Consider a Prep Course

If you didn't pass, you might benefit from a specialized exam prep course. These courses are designed to help you understand the exam format and cover all the material you'll be tested on.

Career Planning

Setting Goals

Whether you passed or not, this is a good time to think about your career goals. What do you hope to achieve in your real estate career? Setting clear, achievable goals will give you something to strive for.

Networking

Start building your professional network as soon as possible. Attend industry events, join real estate associations, and connect with experienced agents who can offer valuable insights.

Marketing Yourself

As a real estate agent, you're essentially running your own business. This means you'll need to market yourself effectively to attract clients. Consider creating a website, setting up social media profiles, and even running ads to get your name out there.

Financial Planning

Real estate can be a lucrative career, but it's also unpredictable. Financial planning is crucial, especially when you're just starting. Make sure you have a financial cushion to cover your expenses until you start closing deals.

Legal Considerations

Contracts and Agreements

As you start practicing, you'll be dealing with various contracts and agreements. Make sure you understand the legal implications of these documents and consult a lawyer if needed.

Ethics and Conduct

Maintaining high ethical standards is crucial in real estate. Familiarize yourself with the Code of Ethics and Standards of Practice of the National Association of Realtors (NAR) and adhere to them strictly.

Conclusion

The period following the New Jersey Real Estate License Exam is crucial for setting the stage for your career. Whether you passed or not, the steps you take now can significantly impact your future success. This chapter has aimed to provide a comprehensive guide to navigate this important phase, from understanding your results to career planning and beyond. Good luck as you embark on this exciting journey in the world of real estate!

Career Development

The journey to becoming a successful real estate agent in New Jersey doesn't end with passing the licensing exam and obtaining your license. In fact, that's just the beginning. This chapter aims to provide an in-depth guide to career development in the real estate industry, covering everything from joining a brokerage to advanced certifications and specializations.

Joining a Brokerage

Why It's Important

As a newly licensed real estate agent, you can't operate independently; you must join a brokerage. The brokerage acts as your business umbrella, providing you with essential resources like MLS access, marketing tools, and legal support.

Types of Brokerages

Traditional Brokerages: These are well-established firms that offer a full range of services and support but usually at the cost of higher commission splits.

Discount Brokerages: These firms offer fewer services but allow you to keep a larger portion of your commission.

Virtual Brokerages: These are online-based firms that offer flexible schedules and lower overhead costs.

What to Look For

Commission Splits: Understand how the commission will be divided between you and the brokerage.

Training Programs: As a newbie, you'll benefit from a brokerage that offers robust training programs.

Cultural Fit: The brokerage's culture should align with your own work style and career goals.

Building a Client Base

Importance of Networking

Networking is the lifeblood of a real estate career. The more people you know, the more likely you are to get client referrals.

Methods

Social Media: Use platforms like Facebook, Instagram, and LinkedIn to connect with potential clients.

Local Events: Attend community events, real estate seminars, and open houses to meet people and hand out your business cards.

Client Referrals: Satisfied clients are your best advocates. Always ask for a referral after a successful deal.

Marketing and Branding

Personal Brand

Your personal brand is what sets you apart from other agents. Work on building a brand that reflects your unique skills and market focus.

Digital Marketing

Website: Create a professional website that showcases your listings, client testimonials, and blog posts.

SEO: Use Search Engine Optimization to make your website more visible on Google.

Email Marketing: Regularly send out newsletters with market updates, tips, and your latest listings.

Traditional Marketing

Flyers and Postcards: These can be distributed in your target neighborhoods.

Billboards and Bench Ads: These are more expensive but can be very effective for brand visibility.

Advanced Certifications and Specializations

Why It's Important

Advanced certifications can make you more attractive to specific types of clients and can justify charging higher commissions.

Types of Certifications:

CRS (Certified Residential Specialist)

ABR (Accredited Buyer's Representative)

SRES (Seniors Real Estate Specialist)

Financial Planning

Budgeting

Real estate income is unpredictable, especially when you're starting. Create a budget that accounts for periods of low income.

Retirement Planning

Consider setting up a retirement account specifically for self-employed individuals, like a SEP IRA or Solo 401(k).

Legal and Ethical Considerations

Importance

Maintaining high ethical standards is not only the right thing to do but also crucial for long-term success.

Common Legal Issues

Disclosure Requirements: Always disclose any known issues with a property to avoid legal problems down the line.

Contractual Obligations: Make sure you fully understand all contracts you enter into.

Conclusion

Career development in real estate is a continuous process that goes far beyond obtaining a license. From choosing the right brokerage to advanced certifications, each decision you make contributes to your long-term success. This chapter has aimed to provide a comprehensive guide to help you navigate the complexities of building a rewarding career in New Jersey's real estate market. With dedication, continuous learning, and a focus on ethical practice, the sky's the limit for what you can achieve.

Conclusion

As we reach the conclusion of this comprehensive guide, "New Jersey Real Estate Learning - New Jersey Real Estate License Exam: Best Test Prep Book to Help You Get Your License!", it's time to pause and reflect on the journey you've embarked upon. From understanding the intricacies of the New Jersey real estate market to diving deep into legal and ethical considerations, this book has aimed to be your all-encompassing resource for succeeding in the real estate industry in New Jersey.

The Importance of Preparation

We've covered a lot of ground, emphasizing the importance of preparation at every step. Whether you're just starting to consider a career in real estate or you're on the cusp of taking your licensing exam, preparation is the key to your success. The chapters on eligibility criteria, the application process, and the exam format were designed to give you a clear roadmap, eliminating any guesswork and setting you up for success.

Beyond the Exam

But this book isn't just about passing an exam; it's about building a fulfilling and successful career. The chapters on career development, specialty areas, and financial planning were included to ensure that you have the tools to thrive in the long term. Real estate is a dynamic and ever-changing field that requires continuous learning and adaptation. The strategies and insights provided in these chapters will serve you well as you navigate the complexities of the real estate world.

The Human Element

Let's not forget the human element in real estate. The chapters on laws of agency, fiduciary duties, and ethics serve as a reminder that real estate is not just about property; it's about people.

Building trust, maintaining ethical standards, and serving your clients' best interests are the cornerstones of a successful real estate career.

Your Next Steps

As you close this book, you're not just ending a reading journey; you're stepping into a new chapter of your professional life. Whether your next step is to submit your license application, take the exam, or perhaps start your first day at a brokerage, remember that every step is a learning opportunity.

A Lifelong Learning Curve

The real estate industry offers a lifelong learning curve. Even the most experienced agents and brokers will tell you that they learn something new with every transaction. This book is your starting point, but don't let your learning curve flatten out. Attend seminars, take advanced courses, and always keep an eye on market trends.

Thank You

Finally, a heartfelt thank you for choosing this book as your guide. Your success is our success, and we wish you all the best in your real estate endeavors in New Jersey. May your career be fulfilling, your transactions smooth, and your clients satisfied. Here's to your future in real estate—may it be as grand as the finest property you'll ever sell!

Final Words

In the ever-evolving landscape of real estate, staying updated and continuously learning are not just options but necessities. This book aimed to equip you with the foundational knowledge and advanced strategies you'll need, but the rest is up to you. Take the initiative, be proactive, and don't hesitate to take those bold steps forward. Your dream career in real estate is not just a possibility; it's a guarantee if you put in the work.

Thank you for reading, and here's to your success in the New Jersey real estate market!

Made in the USA
Middletown, DE
29 August 2024

59975357R00139